CW00429757

Death
by
CIVILISATION

Death by CIVILISATION

How to accidentally ruin a perfectly decent society
(and how it might still be saved)

JAMES CARY

DARTON·LONGMAN + TODD

First published in 2013 by
Darton, Longman and Todd Ltd
1 Spencer Court
140 – 142 Wandsworth High Street
London SW18 4JJ

© 2013 James Cary

The right of James Cary to be identified as the Author of this work
has been asserted in accordance with the Copyright, Designs and
Patents Act 1988.

ISBN 978-0-232-52992-0

With thanks to *Third Way* magazine in which many of these
chapters first appeared.

A catalogue record for this book is available from the British
Library.

Phototypeset by Kerrypress Ltd, Luton, Bedfordshire
Printed and bound by Bell & Bain, Glasgow

For Melissa

Contents

Contents

Contents

Contents

Introduction

Moderation Nation: Why Hitler Couldn't be British and The Solidarity of Stupidity

'The end of the human race will be that it will eventually die of civilization.'
Ralph Waldo Emerson

Moderation Nation

Britain is a nation of moderates. We have never had a true revolution. Not a proper one. A revolution is a furious multitude of the great unwashed storming the palace of the rich and powerful, or throwing secret police files from the rooftops of Stasi Headquarters. It's sudden, violent and dramatic. This is not the British way.

We've had a few civil wars. The Wars of the Roses were mainly toffs and barons charging at each other with private armies. The English Civil War was exactly that: Civil. There were brutal battles, but at the end, the King was not captured, and lynched by an angry mob. He was politely decapitated in Whitehall – famously allowed to wear two shirts to stop his shivering looking like nerves. How British to be deferential and nice to the King, even when you're about to cut off his head.

This great decapitation was done by an act of Parliament, of course, which made it all okay. And then it was all undone by another act of Parliament a decade later. But it was still all okay.

So why no proper revolution? A notable historian called Peter Sibley has a theory. I should point out that this man is not notable for being an historian. He was Captain of Bath Rugby Club in the 1960s. Many years later, he ended up being my history teacher at Monkton Combe School. But his thoughts on the subject of Britain's lack of revolution are still compelling. He puts forward the Drizzle Theory. At key moments in British history, he argues, it has drizzled. It's a convincing idea. A fine rain really puts a dampener on things, even a rioting rabble.

Sibley's case rests mainly on events on 10 April 1848 when Europe was rife with revolutionary fervour. The reformist mass-movement of the day, the Chartists, had gathered in Westminster with their petitions for electoral reform. Incendiary speechmakers were on hand to whip the crowd into a frenzy to ensure their demands were heard. The Prime Minister, aka the Duke of Wellington, was so worried by the scale of the demonstration that he had hidden cannon on Westminster Bridge, Mr Sibley told me, and stocked up on grapeshot to turn a marauding mass into a bloody mess at his command. The stage was set for a revolution.

Events seemed to be coming to a head. The petition was delivered. The crowd became restless. Could this be the moment when the proletariat poured into the Palace of Westminster and declared a new republic based on universal suffrage?

Perhaps it might have done. But it didn't. Because it rained. Everyone ran for cover. You can't rage against the machine when you're struggling to put up an umbrella. And so the revolution had been delayed. Rain stopped play pending further inspection. An early tea was taken. And then, being Britain, everyone left early to beat the traffic. Another revolution avoided.

In Britain, moderation normally wins. Whether it is due to rain, or the feeling of regularly being rained on or our national embarrassment at rather pushily having the word 'Great' in the title of our nation is hard to prove. We do not have revolutions.

Nor do we tend to elect extremists. Most of our political leaders are moderates who fall over themselves to appeal to as many people as possible, posing as your mate in the pub claiming to understand you. And now every election has tiresome pictures of a brainy Oxbridge-type in a bad suit trying to look at home in the Wetherspoons pub nearest his constituency home. It's truly toe-curling.

Why Hitler Couldn't Be British

And yet we are moderates. So we would rather have an uncomfortable policy-wonk sipping a pint of bitter talking about Child Tax Credit than a steely uniformed idealist standing up and telling us how to ruthlessly pursue our national destiny. That kind of rhetoric doesn't play in Britain. Playing a parody of an academic in a sketch, Stephen Fry asks a genuinely good question: 'If Hitler had been British, would we, under similar circumstances, have been moved, charged up, fired up by his inflammatory speeches, or would we simply have laughed?' One suspects we would have done the latter. In P. G. Wodehouse, we read how Bertie Wooster and his friends do not find Roderick Spode and his fascist Blackshorts inspiring, inflammatory or even dangerous but rather laughable and, worst of all, embarrassing. The British would just like people to be nice. Or at least decent, which is a frostier, stand-offish variation of nice.

In our quest to be civilised, we have erected numerous institutions to bring about some kind of niceness or decency. We browbeat our Government into passing laws to make us play nicely. The Media delights in telling us when people aren't being nice so we can all tut or tweet them insults. We ask our Academies to explain why we were born with various genetic dispositions of not-niceness – and how we can fix them. The much-reviled City claims it's trying to generate the cash to pay for all of the above and so there's a limit to how nice they can be. And, on the rare occasions we ask the Church anything, we are generally given a nice Jesus encouraging us to be nice.

All of the above can work well together to produce some moments when we all burst with pride. From the opening ceremony of the London 2012 Olympics until about half way through the closing ceremony, the nation felt a rare moment of pride as the benefits of institutions came together. On the licence-fee funded, non-profit BBC, we watched a superbly-run Olympic games with British athletes romping home with an embarrassment of medals thanks to some state funding, some private sponsorship, the appliance of sport science and some grim determination. And when Clare Balding interviewed them afterwards, they weren't just decent. They were nice. The institutions were firing on all cylinders.

Are You Sitting Comfortably? Well, Don't.

And yet a year earlier, Britain was not nice. It certainly was not a nation 'at ease with itself'. There were riots, originally caused by opaque procedures following a police shooting in Tottenham. Soon there were real angry mobs in a number of cities.

But they were not idealistic readers of Robespierre. They were not trying to smash the system. They were content with smashing the window of Currys Digital to make off with a flat screen TV. These events were isolated, but gave the nation a nasty scare for a week or so. The institutions that were supposed to prevent this sort of thing stared at each other in stupefied amazement. How did that happen?

The police were blamed for inciting the event and handling it poorly; the politicians were blamed for failing to provide jobs and services; the city was blamed for the financial downturn. The riots petered out. Questions were asked. The media got bored, moved on and then imploded with the collapse of the *News of The World*, links to the police and politicians, and there were more concerns that our institutions were corrupt or compromised. And then the BBC imploded. Again.

Why Are You Telling Me This?

All of the above brings me to the book you currently hold in your hands. On first inspection, it appears to be a ragbag selection of pieces on anything and everything. A closer inspection may reveal the same conclusion. But as the writer of these pieces I have noticed that whenever I approach a subject, I come back to same question again and again. The question is this: Why are we so convinced that institutions will save us, when they are more likely to enslave us?

It seems alarmist to say such a thing, especially in a nice, moderate place like Britain. But the world is a graveyard of collapsed empires that believed themselves to be every bit as sophisticated and civilised are we do today. The world has been dominated by the most unlikely of tribes: The Egyptians, The Greeks, The Mongols, The Italians, The Turks, The Spanish, The Portuguese, The Dutch, the self-effacing Brits, The Germans and Japanese, briefly, and The Americans. But the problem with great, sprawling empires is that they often collapse under the weight of their own civilisation.

An archaeologist will get out his trowel to show you a palace that's been left as a ruin. An anthropologist will find entire cities that have been deserted. But why? Occasionally, the weather or a new disease is to blame. But normally it's an ossified system that is unable to cope with being blindsided by change. Institutions that were created to bring about greatness became robust, but then hardened, became brittle and shattered into a thousand pieces. Mighty leaders proved to have feet of clay, toppling over and taking everyone down with them.

The collapse of a society always seems unthinkable, and yet history tells us it happens to all civilisations and empires.

Unhappy Easter

Let us look at the example of Easter Island, the story of a people who built nearly four hundred astonishingly large stone statues. How could a sophisticated society commit collective suicide by eating all the food and chopping down all the trees?

If we're being kind, maybe we'd put the blame on finite natural resources, or evil Westerners, but this does not explain how a population should suddenly fall from 15,000 to 2000 in a brutal bloodbath.

The theory is that the islanders were not one single happy tribe living in perfect harmony, but a group of competitive clans who occupied various sections of the Island. It almost feels like one of those board-games designed by a bespectacled German. Each clan on Easter Island had a greater share of one of the resources they needed to build these large statues: rock, for the statues themselves; wood, for the statues' movement and mounting; and food, to feed the people involved. Their shared goals of 'Let's see who can build the biggest statue' got them trading with each other.

But the soil became exhausted (it was never that great in the first place) and all the trees had been cut down (these things didn't grow very fast with the rough soil and indifferent climate). For years, anthropologists were reluctant to believe that humans, especially lovely Polynesians could have turned on each other in their quest to continue building their statues that served no actual purpose. Surely they would have realised that building statues to show off to each other was so self-destructive that it would have been stopped before there was a resources melt-down? Surely they weren't so stupid as to cut down *all* their trees – which would mean the end of statue production, fuel for fires and cooking, material for canoes and any possible means of escape from the Island in wooden boats?

Sadly, the Easter Islanders proved themselves to be no different from the rest of humanity. They really were that stupid.

The Solidarity of Stupidity

A revolution happened, but it was too late. Statue building stopped. They turned on their own gods when they failed to deliver more wood and food and went around tipping over their own, and possibly each other's, statues. There was in-fighting, starvation and cannibalism. There is evidence in many societies that people resort to cannibalism before the food runs out. When anthropologists had the bright idea of asking modern Easter Islanders what they thought happened to their ancestors, they were quick to confirm tales of cannibalism. The worst taunt you could say to an enemy on the island apparently was 'The flesh of your mother sticks between my teeth'. Not nice. But revealing.

However grim the tale of Easter Island is, their collective idiocy is not all that surprising. If you were to drop one of them into Northern Europe in 1917, they would be appalled. If you were to explain to them why millions of men were mechanically mowing each other down with machine guns, they wouldn't know whether to laugh or cry. Verdun is perfectly nice town, but not a place worth fighting over – at least not with anything more than fisticuffs. And yet armed, immovable, unstoppable European states converged in a way that made it seem worth the lives of 300,000 French and German soldiers. The twentieth century is sadly littered with such examples. Millions of bodies.

Bad Parenting

The problem is that if you predict such calamity, or even warn against such dangers, you will be laughed at. Let us take an example from the Bible. In the Old Testament, the Israelites are in the desert and about to enter the Promised Land. Moses warned them about what might happen in the future in that land. He tells them not to imitate the religions of people they find there – because they might end up sacrificing their children to these gods in a fire. Not metaphorically. Literally. Look it up in Deuteronomy 18.

Imagine hearing this warning. You'd look at Moses, and then your children and say 'I don't think this one is aimed at me. In fact, I can't see who it is aimed at. What kind of maniac is going to sacrifice their own children to anything or anyone?' And yet turn on a few pages and the Israelites did turn to these gods and took part in child sacrifice. Moses had sounded insane, but knew what religious system humans were capable of creating when they got together. And so he issued the warning – but his warnings fell on deaf, complacent ears.

Seriously, Why Are You Telling Me This?

I am not claiming to be Moses, or any kind of voice in the wilderness. I am not a prophet or a son of a prophet. I am, in fact, the son of a dairy farmer. But if you don't believe the son of a farmer, or Moses, listen to the words of Walter Bagehot who wrote, 'The whole history of civilisation is strewn with creeds and institutions which were invaluable at first, and deadly afterwards.'

And this is my overall point throughout the book. Institutions get in the way and if you don't stop them, change them, challenge them or pull them down in good time, they will ruin society. And so this book is divided into five sections, each containing chapters about a great institution or collection thereof; The Media; The Economy; The State; Academia; and The Church.

I don't expect anyone to listen or take me seriously. That's fine. I am used to being ignored: I have children. I understand that the chapters in this book may appear to be the writings of a madman. But it may just be that this madman is slightly less mad than everyone else.

Part One:
The Media, the Arts and all things Cultural

'Television is an invention that permits you to be entertained in your living room by people you wouldn't have in your home.'
Sir David Frost

After much thought, it seemed a pity to start this book with chapters about politics and the State. It would be such a shame to fall out so early in our relationship. And so let us begin by holding up a mirror to the all-seeing-eye that is the media.

The British media never ceases to amaze and disappoint. The media is never happier than talking about itself. During the Jimmy Savile scandal, many of us will have been exposed to the ultimate media feedback loop: *Channel 4 News* correspondents discussing the episode of *Panorama* about *Newsnight's* dropping of the story about a deceased BBC employee and professional weirdo and how ITV ran the story as a documentary instead.

Mercifully, there is more in this section than chapters about television. We also examine festivals, biopics, books, horse racing, Twitter, piracy and why it's perfectly okay to make jokes about the French.

An Exercise in Finger-pointing

or: Why the Leveson Inquiry was like a Tarantino movie (minus the swearing)

It was a key turning point in the programme's history and demonstrated that something had to change. When Christine Hamilton took the moral high ground over Angus Deayton on *Have I Got News For You?*, it was clear that his position was untenable. Similarly, the Leveson Inquiry provided stables for a number of high horses on which the likes of Steve Coogan and Hugh Grant have been more than happy to trot out of. By their own admission, Mssrs Coogan and Grant are hardly blameless saints. But when men such as these are given the opportunity to call someone else's ethics into question, you know that things have gone badly wrong.

But things are even worse than that. These celebrities were given this chance by a Parliament which had recently seen a handful of its own members sent to prison for criminally fiddling their expenses. And all of the above are reported on by the media that refers to 'the media' as something that doesn't include themselves. All in all, this is almost the very definition of the expression 'media merry-go-round'. Drug-taking adulterous celebrities have been taking the moral high-ground on a criminally intrusive media in front of an assembled committee of implied fraudsters. It feels like a scene from a Tarantino movie, in which everyone is screaming, terrified, furious and pointing a gun at everyone else.

How has this happened? Who is to blame? Ultimately, the people to blame are the sort of people who write 'Who is to blame?' As well as the sort of people who want to hear an answer to the question 'Who is to blame?' And the sort of people who don't want that answer to be in any way complicated. That would be 'us'.

We don't want complexity, and we've managed to construct a popular media that no longer exposes us to it. We live in a culture of headlines. If a news story is hard to explain, it doesn't exist. And so headlines *are* the story. If you've got a story about a complex fraud case, forget it. If you've got a story about ethnic clashes in Africa with no clear villains, you really don't have a hope. Headlines control the agenda. We've known for many years that we live in the age of the soundbite, and this is the cost.

We've come to expect interesting headlines. That's why I had to think of some so you'd be interested in reading this chapter of a book you'd already bought. In fact, I came up with two titles. One nice short intriguing one, 'An Exercise in Finger-pointing', and a comically unwieldy title that would hopefully draw you into this piece, designed to reassure you that although the piece is about the Leveson Inquiry, it's interesting and funny.

Every story needs a headline. And it's much more likely to be run on the front page or find its way to the front of the broadcast if it's got a snappy and surprising headline. The trouble is, if headlines are your idol you'll do anything to get them, including going through the bins of celebrities, hiding in bushes with a long-lens camera and hacking into the voicemail of a missing teenager. Hence, the Leveson Inquiry.

But let us work through a fairly tame, hypothetical example to see the effect of headlines for the narrative of the story. Let's say a train crashes causing the death of several people. But one is a girl called, say, Lucy who is in her twenties and mercifully photogenic. There are lots of pictures of her on her Facebook page looking gorgeous which will reinforce the narrative that her pretty carefree life has been tragically cut short. This would be an irresistible one for the immensely popular *Daily Mail*.

Here come the headline writers. What are the options? Let's start with: 'Who killed lovely Lucy?' in shrieking black letters. This, of course, implies that one single person is responsible. So the question goes out: Who was the driver and what on *earth* did he think he was doing? Answer: Let us assume the driver tried to do the job he was trained for and doesn't have a death wish. If we look at the evidence, we'll see there was a signal problem. So that headline is not going to help.

Could there be a pleasing play on words: 'Sending the Wrong Signal'? So the question goes out: Who fitted those signals and where do they live so we can turn up with pitchforks and a lynch mob? Answer: Let us assume that the publicly listed company who fitted those signals have strict procedures and routinely test them. Something probably went wrong with that.

Could we make this about money too? 'Fat Cat gets the cream while Foxy Lucy pays the price'? You'd need a broadsheet to run that one. In which case the question goes out: Okay, so how much do the idiots who run that company make? And how big is their bonus? Answer: Corporate pay is a pressing but separate issue. The reality is that the rail system is an historically underfunded and complex network of relationships that throws up anomalies and discrepancies that I can tell from your body language do not interest you.

If you have a pre-determined, headline-driven narrative, your article will over-simplify the complexities of life in order to fit into a pre-conceived story-arc. And worse still, that story is *already* a cliché, e.g. 'Rags to riches musician has alcohol/drug problem'. That's the big irony in all this. The idol is not worth the sacrifice. Now there's a surprise.

The Fine Line between Comedy and Tragedy

or: Why sitcoms are incredibly moralistic (and that's okay)

There are plenty of commentators and columnists who look around the world and see nothing but moral decline. They point to the 'breakdown' of things they like and the 'rise' of things they don't like. Is society any less moral than it ever was? Times are changing. (I did originally type 'a-changing', but then deleted the 'a-' because it felt old-fashioned somehow). In past times, we used to venerate the old and overlook the young. These days we dump our old people in homes but wrap our children in cotton wool.

No one needs to be more aware of these socially agreed mores than the sitcom writer because, strange as it may seem, sitcoms are intensely moral. In a way, everything under the sun has a moral dimension, but sitcoms are so blatantly moralistic that we no longer notice it.

Ancient Greece had Aesop's fables. Jesus told parables. In Medieval times, they had mystery plays. Today, we have the sitcom – artificially neat, half-hour comedies about a bunch of characters all with conflicting quests and desires that conveniently begin and end within about 72 hours. Crucially, the characters never learn or change their behaviour. Next week, they'll make the same mistakes again. In this sense, sitcoms closely resemble real life. We don't change – and nor do our friends, neighbours and relatives. All good sitcoms are based on this solid truth (and plenty of bad ones).

But there is another key truth to the sitcom – a strong sense of justice. I reflected on this when thinking about *Derek*, Ricky Gervais' new comedy drama (Dramedy? Coma?). In sitcoms, your characters need two things. The first is character flaws. They need to have a problem with their personality that means they are craving something they lack. In Captain Mainwaring's case, it's the respect of his men. In Alan B'Stard's case, it's power. In David Brent's case, it's the undying admiration of his colleagues. These are all understandable flaws but crucially they are *culpable*. When they fall flat on their faces, we don't feel too sorry for them because they should know better – and they don't listen to advice. Or they listen to the wrong advice. They can be blamed for their failings. This is important.

The second thing a lead character needs is a clear quest each week – a plan to win that respect or power or admiration. Their culpable flaws hamstring their attempts, so hilarious calamity can ensue. But at the back of the audience's mind is the overarching worry about whether the character deserves their calamity. The eponymous character in *Derek*, despite the public statements of Ricky Gervais, is clearly someone with severe learning difficulties. He was born with them. And this is a character flaw for which he is not to blame. He doesn't deserve calamity. Not in sitcom-land.

Being a massively successful, gong-collecting, multi-millionaire, Gervais knows all this. This is why nothing bad happened to Derek in *Derek*, because he didn't deserve it. So the programme ended up being sentimental rather than funny – which is fine if you like that sort of thing. It would have been nice to have seen something bad happen to Derek's mate, the caretaker, who was culpably mean about the old people living in the home. He deserved a good kicking.

Perhaps this is the difference between comedy and tragedy. In comedy, the ending is a happy one because people get their just deserts. In tragedy, the ending is sad because justice is not done – the good are thwarted and the evil prosper – or a character was unable to change to prevent their final demise.

Comedy is surely the more satisfying of the two and yet there is a strong popular appetite for tragedy. I can't bear it, myself. Give me P. G. Wodehouse over Evelyn Waugh any day. On holiday a few years ago, I was reading about the adventures of Crouchback in one of Evelyn Waugh's *Sword of Honour* books and ended up screaming 'Just leave the poor man alone!' Bad things were happening to our hero that he simply didn't deserve.

The problem is that every day we hear stories of bad things happening to good people. Lumps are found where there shouldn't be lumps. Crucial documents go astray. Floods sweep away villages. Tragedy may describe our human experience – but not our aspiration, and deep-seated instinct about how the universe should be. Maybe that's the appeal of the sitcom – not just the jokes, the characters or farcical situations, but a world in which the proud are humbled, the greedy are impoverished and the meek inherit the earth. Sounds familiar.

Betrayed by Delia

or: Why TV chefs don't actually teach you how to cook

I can still remember the night when I turned on the television and saw it happen. It was like seeing Bob Dylan playing with an electric blues band at the Newport Folk Festival in 1965 when fans booed as their idol appeared to be turning his back on his folk roots. But I was not watching a crime against music, but a felony against food. I sat dumbstruck as Delia reached into a store cupboard and pulled out a tin of minced beef. Let me repeat that. A tin. Of minced beef.

A further body blow came as she plucked some frozen mash from the freezer, as bold as brass, to make the topping for a shepherd's pie (like mash is really hard work). I then lurched as I assumed the world was no longer spinning on its axis. Delia, the nation's unofficial cooking tsar, had sold out. My wife and I booed the television.

We expected better. Yes, sure, I have purchased some tinned meat before – and not just corned beef. The tinned steak from M&S is delicious in a pie with some chopped carrots and onions. But I don't expect this sort of thing from Delia. It'd be like Kirstie Allsop buying a jumper from the Edinburgh Woollen Mill, rather than spinning the yarn, knitting it herself and entering it into a competition at an agricultural show.

I suppose I had already betrayed Delia. I had been two-timing, well, four-timing her with Jamie, Hugh and Gordon. I have not been five-timing her. I've never really warmed to Heston's approach but he is a key member of the grub squad at Channel 4.

It's an odd phenomenon, really. Channel 4 likes to be achingly cool and prides itself on giving platforms to minorities, marginalised voices and alternative views. And yet its five main cooking brands are middle-aged white men who ruthlessly exploit their media profile to make mountains of money. Having said that, none of these men seem interested in money – or even food itself – despite the fact they're all TV chefs. Allow me to explain.

Let's begin with Hugh Fearnley-Whittingstall, expensively educated, double-barrelled and terribly well-spoken. His quest for fresh food continually unearths extraordinary-looking older whiter men with strange beards, bad hair and terrible teeth. And the occasional middle-aged lady who makes jam or dressings out of acorns. Hugh's friends could not be less hip. But for him it's all about the food. Natural, organic, home-grown or wild, and above all, seasonal. He seems to have a hotline to Mother Nature herself, if she existed (she doesn't). He is essentially a pagan, a title Hugh would probably not eschew. But Hugh also celebrates the abundance of nature, which Christians should also celebrate. God didn't just make plants, but seed-bearing ones. He created seasons and, try as we might, *we* can't actually make anything grow.

But will Hugh fill the Delia void and teach you how to cook? Not really. Unless you can butcher your own pigs, grow your own junipers, and deep-fry your own parsnip crisps in hemp oil.

You could try some cooking along with Gordon Ramsay, a man with more pent-up energy than a loaded, cocked blunderbuss. But for him, it's not really about cooking or food, either. Gordon is about excellence. Bad food physically offends him. Badly-run restaurants send him into fits of rage. Food must be as good as it can be – and turn a profit. Ultimately, he's not pagan, like Hugh, but a proponent of the Protestant work ethic. (Maybe he picked it up at Rangers.) But unless you want to learn how to make a Caesar salad at knifepoint (which perhaps he also picked up at Rangers), I wouldn't ask him for cooking lessons.

Don't even bother with Heston Blumenthal. Let's face it. He's not a chef; he's a chemist. That's not a bad thing. It's fascinating television. And I'm sure his restaurants take your breath away (they then supercool that breath, dip it in liquid nitrogen and coat it in sugar and serve it as a very light pudding). For Heston, food should be a multi-sensory experience. If one needs a conical flask to make scrambled eggs, so be it. And if those eggs taste better with plum jam and oxtail, then he'll put them all together on a muffin (cooked on a Bunsen burner, naturally with garlic butter made in a fume cupboard). So unless you have access to your child's chemistry set, cooking with Heston will be a frustrating affair.

For proper cooking lessons, we must to turn to Jamie Oliver who'd like to teach the world to cook. With the passion of John Wesley, he tried to convert the whole of Rotherham to home-cooked classics and crusaded to improve school dinners. But for him, it's not just about food preparation and eating well. It's not just about being in tune with the seasons, executing meals to perfection or drying your salad in the Hadron Collider – food is about people. Cooking together. Eating together. Being together. It's a thoroughly biblical view of food. He is surely right to point out that what you eat and how you eat it affects how you live and how your kids behave and relate to others. After all, what hope do we have of any kind of national, or even ecclesiastical, unity when many of us eat bad convenience salty fatty food all alone? And with Our Lady Delia of the Tinned Goods teaching us how to make meals from bags and tins, Jamie may just be the lone voice in the wilderness.

Summer Reading

or: Books to pack before you knock off on holiday

Before you slope off to the beach, villa or gite, make sure you have plenty to read. Allow me to recommend some treats currently on offer.

New Fiction

The Saharan Sparrow – Volume Press (£6.99)

The briefly-awaited fourteenth novel in The Gambian Detective Bureau for Older Women series. Jonathon McGill-Jones tells a charming tale of a sparrow that gets into Phillis Njie's church and it doesn't want to leave. The local vicar seems happy with the situation but there is more to this than meets the eye. But not much. Voted by *Good Living* magazine as 'The book most likely to be given to a women in her mid-late thirties.'

A Hundred Moons a Year – Kandahar Press (£12.99)

A small boy in a war-torn country finds a small telescope and dreams of becoming an astronaut and going to the moon. He doesn't make it, but he learns a lot of other stuff besides that's almost as good. Critically acclaimed, but mainly because only critics have time to read it. (It's 800 pages – there's a whole generational sub-plot story that goes on a bit.) Voted by the *London Review of Books* as 'The book you're most likely to lie about reading.'

iMam – Crescent Press (£8.99)

A romantic comedy by Saf Khan about Adil, a twenty-something Muslim trainee imam who strikes up a friendship with an American girl who introduces him to the music of Jimi Hendrix. Unfortunately, he is found listening to it on an iPod in the mosque during prayers and his life, and career, start to unravel. After a series of contrivances, a cricket match, the wedding of a relative and lots of family pressure, he is forced to choose between Allah and Purple Haze. Somehow, he gets both. Pastel-coloured pulp meets Islam. About time. 'Avoid' – *Islamabad Echo*.

New Non-Fiction

Split-Second by Simon Gladmore – Tenuous Books (£8.99)

In the blinking of an eye, we make split-second decisions that impact not only our own lives but those of others. Sounds obvious. It is. But read all about it over several hundred pages with a few graphs thrown in to make it look academic. And find out how the divorce rate is linked to the disappearance of the Amazonian Golden Tree Frog. Voted by the Cosmo Awards as 'The Book most Likely to be Read Exclusively by Men.'

Life in the Freezer by Delia Smith – BBC Cash-In (£15.99)

The nation's favourite cook explains how to live exclusively on frozen food. Yes, Delia's gone to Iceland. And she's loving it. Discounts available if bought with *Life in a Can* by Delia Smith.

Gordon's Square Meals by Gordon Ramsay – Effing Media (£20.99)

On top of his seven restaurants, TV programmes in the UK and US and a column in a weekend newspaper, is there any chance this celebrity chef has actually had anything to do with the contents of this book? 'Nice pictures, though,' *What Pastry Cutter? Magazine*.

War on Error by Sally Trust – Pedantrix Press (£8.99)

Being a terrorist doesn't mean you have to drop your punctuation. Sally Trust casts a watchful eye over the grammatical errors of modern times, including a humour chapter on Al-Qaeda and other paramilitary groups, and wonders how these young men ever made it through school without knowing the difference between a comma and a full stop. This book follows her previous hit *Catastrophe Apostrophe: How Flash Floods and Hurricanes Need Not Mean the End of Proper Syntax.*

New Religion

I'm Sure There Might Be a God by Jim Hounslow – BBC Legible (£12.99)

Hardened by years of reportage and politics, Jim Hounslow comes out as an agnostic and pretends to have an open mind about religion for most of the book, before returning to his original thesis that religions disagree with each other and cause wars so there's probably nothing in it. 'Read the first two chapters and you get the general gist.' *The Book Review.*

The New Perspective on Pauline Eschatology in the Latter Part of the Acts of the Apostles: A Response by former Archbishop Rowan Williams.

This book is probably very good and insightful. But we will never know. The blurb says Williams questions the role of law, temple theology and sacrificial worship within pre-Christian mainstream Jewish practice. We'll have to take his word for it. 'I couldn't even work out which way up it was mean to go' *Theology Today.* 'Even by my standards, this is a little complex.' Bishop Tom Wright.

New History

Nazis: The Truth by Lawrence Rhys – Same Again Press (£11.99)

A detailed look at the Nazi propaganda machine, the Gestapo and the SS. In case you needed reminding, the Nazis were vile and reading about them gives you a warm feeling of superiority.

Also, from Old Rope Books: *Instructions to Australian Servicemen in Sicily; Instructions to Indian Servicemen in Austria; Instructions to Irishmen Servicemen in Ireland.*

A Short History of Coriander by Giles Fenton – (£8.99)

A book about the history of the human progress which, apparently, hinged on the trade of coriander. Without it, Fenton says Henry VIII would have died as an infant, Faraday would never have discovered electricity and Armstrong would certainly not have walked on the moon (it would have been Buzz Aldrin). This all comes as a surprise because Fenton's last book argued that everything hinged on the discovery of star anise.

Happy reading!

A Day at the Races

or: How Michael Barrymore turned me against dancing

There are two things that I'm prepared to admit that I am prejudiced against: Dancing and Horse Racing. There is a simple reason for this. Both of these things were unwelcome intrusions into my childhood desire to watch little else on TV except comedy and cricket. Allow me to explain.

I've always loved comedy and growing up in the 1980s there wasn't that much stand-up comedy on television. We didn't have *Live At the Apollo* back then. On the BBC, there was Little and Large who, to be fair, at least had the 'Harry Secombe's Car Starting' routine. On ITV there was the likeable Cannon and Ball, but both acts were, let's be honest, a lengthy reminder of just how good Morecambe and Wise were. If you wanted edgier stand-up comedy you had to stay up for Dave Allen or Jasper Carrott, which was superb.

If you wanted more stand-up, you had to wait for a *Live at the Palladium* or a Royal Variety Show to come round. I would sit excitedly on the floor, waiting for the compere (often Jimmy Tarbuck) to announce the next turn. If the next act were a dance troupe, rather than Michael Barrymore (yes, you liked him too), I would be sent into convulsions of disappointment. A singer, like Shirley Bassey, I could just about tolerate. But dancing? However beautiful or graceful the dancing is, it is a yawning absence of comedy, which makes me dislike it. It's irrational and childish, but there it is.

In a similar way, horse racing was an unwelcome intrusion into my viewing of international test cricket. David

Gower, my cricketing hero, may have been about to score a century against Australia (in fact in 1985 he scored a blissful 215), but we had to go over to Haydock Park to see if Hello Dandy would win the 3.30. Dancing and horse racing got in the way of both of my passions. For this, I resent them.

Many years later, I no longer loathe dancing. I like ballet when my four-year-old daughter does it. But that's about my limit. I am immune to its charms, just as I am always left unmoved by the works of U2 and The Cohen Brothers (*Fargo* excepted, obviously).

My hostility to horse racing remains, however, and so I was very heartened when the BBC decided to stop squandering the licence fee on it. Granted this will possibly mean the permanent loss of one of the BBC's greatest asset in Clare Balding. It will also give yet more attention to the one who needs it least – Channel 4's preposterous John McCririck.

Lots of things about horse racing are preposterous, although they are not necessarily arguments against it. Plenty of fine sports are preposterous. A Test Match is gloriously daft, taking five days, stopping for luncheon and tea, and doesn't always reach a conclusion in all that time. Horse racing is similarly ludicrous and at least demonstrates that it does not take itself too seriously. If they allow a name like 'Maythehorsebewithyou' you know this sport is not full of stuffed shirts.

Some of the race names are similarly comic. Calling a race 'The Queen Mother Champion Chase' is just asking people to conjure up images of Her Majesty's mother in a little blue dress and veiled hat being pursued by horses as well as hounds. (It's what she would have wanted.) Curiously-named horses and races, funny hand-gestures and even more curiously-named correspondents, like the BBC's wonderfully named Cornelius Lysaght, are all fine.

In fact, all of these bits of frippery and nonsense distract from the fact that the BBC have been participating in a sporting racket for far too long. Let's be honest. Horse racing is *all* about gambling. Some people say they just love the beautiful horses, but it's not about the horses. The same people who'll talk about a shimmering coat and a horse 'with a sense of humour' will scream and shout for a three-eyed multi-coloured nag if they have ten quid riding on it. The sport is about gambling and the BBC have been completely fine with this, to the point where they give out racing tips on their national BBC radio breakfast shows. Why does the BBC even have a view on how we can make money off the 1.50 from Chepstow? It's not about the horses.

If you're a fan of horses, why make them run races in which they might well fatally injure themselves? A very recent Cheltenham meeting led to the premature deaths of five horses. I'm no horse enthusiast (can you tell?) and even I would shudder at that rate of attrition. Animals that are used in experiments at least contribute to humanity's scientific knowledge. But I'm not sure God made horses so we could ride them to death, whilst betting on who's going to win.

I'm not sure how much a horse is worth – we are, of course, worth more than the sparrows – but if a jockey is worth ten horses, how about every ten horses that die in racing, they have to shoot a jockey? I'm sure safety would improve dramatically.

So I say good riddance to Horse Racing on the BBC. In its place, let's have something more ethical: a live fox hunt. At least it only results in the death of one animal. And it's possibly more ethical than watching misguided hopeless cases be torn apart in front of millions on *The X Factor*.

The Problem of Piracy

or: Why the best things in life are reasonably priced

Contrary to popular belief, the words of Luther aren't true. The best things in life are not free. (I am, of course, referring to Luther Vandross.) For example, NBC's comedy *30 Rock,* starring Tina Fey and Alec Baldwin, is one of the best things in life. And it isn't free. At least it isn't to me. Series 3 on DVD cost me £15.99 from Amazon. One could argue that some of the best things in life can be found for a reasonable price.

Except the best things in life are free somewhere if you look online. In fact, you can listen to Luther Vandross and Janet Jackson sing 'The Best Things in Life are Free' on Spotify. For free. Or it'll be on YouTube somewhere. Admittedly, it's not a truly great song, but there are plenty of good songs out there on the free version of Spotify, bootlegged on YouTube. It's all there.

Except it's not quite free. On Spotify, there are adverts that are frequent, annoying and inappropriate. I can only presume they are designed to encourage you to upgrade to the ad-free premium service. I resisted this encouragement until they imposed limits on how many times you could listen to any track. And once I couldn't listen to *Owner of a Lonely Heart* by Yes any more, I decided to upgrade. And now Rick Wakeman gets a tiny percentage of the £4.99 I pay Spotify every month. It's not a lot, but Spotify would advance two arguments. They would say my exposure to Yes makes me more likely to purchase their music. I'm not sure about this, since I can keep listening to it and everything else as long as I keep paying £4.99. They could also argue that I'm more like to see Yes in concert. This works in theory, although the story of the band Yes is comically complex. At one point the original line-up of Yes were touring, singing their own Yes songs, but weren't allowed to be called Yes because the official Yes were *still* touring. Yes is, in this case, a bad example.

Overall, I now spend about £60 a year on Spotify plus a few pounds here and there on iTunes and the occasional tenner on an album if I'm seeing a lesser-known band live at a gig. Before Spotify, iTunes and broadband internet in general, my annual spending on music was considerably more as I regularly bought albums from HMV. But back then, I didn't have two kids and a mortgage. But even though I spend a lot less now, I still begrudge the £4.99 a month since I'm used to everything on the internet being free.

The problem is that we've been spoiled by getting things free – and it's not just music but TV and Radio. iPlayer is limited in that programmes expire, but it's free. At least it seems so. It isn't, really. Its content and platform is paid for by the licence fee. People outside Britain slightly tilt their heads when you explain to them the concept of the licence fee. When you think about it, it's a weird anomaly. Parliament has granted tax-raising powers to the makers of *Dick and Dom in da Bungalow* and *Eggheads*. And yet the makers of *The X Factor*, *Peep Show* and *Soccer AM* don't have this advantage. But now many of them give away their content for free online as well.

But the tide is turning. Sky's *Soccer AM* isn't being given away. In fact, Rupert Murdoch now charges for *The Times Online*. And the *Telegraph* looks like charging people for its content outside the UK. Media moguls have understood that they can't carry on as they have been. But for all their talk of 'embracing the web as an exciting opportunity', Hollywood and the music industry are still terrified of the internet. Apple have done them a big favour with iTunes and thrown some dollars into the coffers, having taken their bite. TV networks in America have put content on Hulu and

YouTube, whilst packing them with unavoidable adverts in an attempt to claw back their bucks. But the fact is that anyone could find Series 3 of *30 Rock* somewhere on the internet for free. All you need is bandwidth and a five minute tutorial in using Bittorrent. (I still don't understand how it works.)

Technology makes piracy of technology extremely easy. It's so easy that even 'good' people can do it. But this is not new. The equipment has always been there to make copies of copyright material. It always seemed strange to me that Sony have a record label, but have always sold technology that allows you to record things off the radio, and record CDs onto cassette or minidisc. This seems tantamount to giving a random stranger a gun and then acting surprised when they rob you blind.

The other factor that eases our consciences as would-be pirates is that the victims are often wealthy and powerful. It's hard to feel sorry for Bill Gates, or Sting, when using a nicked or unlicensed version of Microsoft Office or listening to 'Fields of Gold' on YouTube. It's hard not to feel preached at when cinemas use loud music to convey the fact that piracy is like shoplifting – when they've charged you £9.20 for a cinema ticket, £4 for a drink and snack and still make you watch 15 minutes of commercials and 15 minutes of trailers. And it's hard to take bands like Metallica seriously when they bypass their hard rock rebel image to say 'Hey, you should ask nicely before borrowing something, especially if it's our music'. But however preposterous Metallica appear to be (which is a lot) they are surely right.

The biggest problem, though, is the anti-piracy messages themselves are watered down. Record labels say 'stealing money from the big acts means that we can't invest in new acts'. Movie studios say 'Buying pirate copies of films funds organised crime.' This is because we live in an age of relativism where it isn't done to state something is simply in itself flat-out wrong or immoral. It's no wonder that piracy is a problem when we need a reason for saying 'stealing is wrong'. While that ethical culture prevails, there's no prospect of stopping piracy.

Twittiquette

or: How to win followers and influence people

Recently, I experienced something of a first. I went on a Twitter date. It was nothing romantic, you understand. Just coffee. But it was with someone that I only know because of Twitter. He's a script guy, and so am I, and we found we regularly saw eye-to-eye on comedy matters out in the Twitterverse, so I suggested we meet up to shoot the breeze. Which we did. Rarely has breeze been so well shot – especially if you define shooting the breeze as moaning that BBC and ITV don't commission enough situation comedy. Which I do. Hence, it was rather fun.

As you can already tell, I am a fan of Twitter. And, like most fans of Twitter, I am defensive about it since the criticisms of this social network are multiple, obvious and, above all, accurate. But let's run through the upsides, the first of which is the gospel of brevity. In an internet era in which more is more, the pages of virtual text pile ever higher. In these garrulous times, the limitation of each tweet to 140 characters ensures pleasingly concise communication. This is long enough to make an interesting point or tell a decent joke, but not so short we're into the realm of the tabloid headline. So, tweets may be a continuous stream of tattle, but it's succinct tattle.

Twitter allows you to voluntarily listen directly and un-filtered to people you find interesting or talented, be they Stephen Fry, Caitlin Moran, Graham Linehan or Ben Golda-cre along with their respective acolytes or critics. You can follow inventive and amusing personae, like Stephen Fry's fictional wife or Giles Coren (who surely doesn't really exist, does he?) You can also subscribe to tweets from your favourite magazines, and those types who are just really good at digging gold out of the huge, mountainous and impenetrable internet.

It's especially fun to watch a high-profile TV programme with Twitter alongside you, as people make various comments and wisecracks. This activity taps into two eternal human characteristics: the first is hurling abuse. (Undoubtedly the first papyrus, printing press, telegram and telephone were used to convey snide remarks and unfair criticism about other forms of media.) The second is our deep human need for relationship. This shouldn't be any surprise, given that we are made in God's image, and that he is profoundly relational, being three persons in communion with Himself.

We were not created to be independent, self-sufficient units. We were made to be in families, communities, tribes and nations. And so when someone invents a new technology that saves us one more trip to the high street or the office, someone else invents another one to help us to say 'hi' to someone we know about as well as a bank teller or the new guy at work. Twitter is just one more way of saying 'notice me' and 'I've had a hard day' as well as 'hey, check out this freak'.

The critics of Twitter and Facebook like to point out that your online contacts are not real friends. At best, they are friends-lite. But this is a willful misunderstanding of online relationships which everyone knows are different from being in the same room as someone. Facebook has 'friends', but Twitter has 'followers'. There is no pretence at a reciprocal relationship – and there is no obligation to 'follow' someone who 'follows' you. If Stephen Fry followed everyone of his followers, his iPhone would surely explode.

There is, of course, the worry that Twitter is just one big, grown-up popularity contest. This isn't a worry. It's a fact. Twitter is one huge global playground and the person with the biggest posse is the winner. Sadly I care about how many followers I have on Twitter – especially in relation to other comedy writers. And so I try not to annoy followers by using it as form of texting or email. For me, Twitter is a work tool that I use specifically for engaging with people about writing, and sitcom in particular (hence my Twitter name is @sitcomgeek).

The only thing that makes me uncomfortable about the term 'followers' is that it crops up in the New Testament to describe disciples of Jesus – who of course took many years to build up more followers than the prophet of our age, Stephen Fry. Jesus only had 12 followers, rising to 72 and then a few thousand (with a serious jump after feeding the five thousand). But Good Friday saw almost everyone 'unfollow' him, leaving only two on Easter Sunday. Thankfully, the gospel writers did not feel the need to sound like West Coast teenagers or @marymagz would have tweeted: 'Jesus alive?!?!! :-0 totes amaze. Mistook him 4 gardener!! LOL!!!' We can be grateful for small mercies.

What to Do With Your Summer

or: Some jokes at the expense of festivals

The summer of 2013 will be an odd one. We have no international football tournament at which to vent our collective disappointment. We have no international athletics tournament at which to acquire a sudden interest in cycling, rowing, archery and modern pentathlon. Wimbledon is only going to take up two weeks. The cinemas will be playing the usual special-effects-fests, with loud bangs hoping to distract you from realising you're watching part 4 of a trilogy. And if you stay at home, you'll find bleak TV schedules, as the channel controllers keep the 'good stuff' back for the autumn. So if you can't face re-watching your *West Wing* boxed set for the sixth time, you'll need to find something else to do. Fortunately, help is at hand, in this guide to getting out and about this summer.

The extraordinary proliferation of literary festivals is brought into question in the *Why-Oh-Why Literary Festival* (sponsored by *The Independent*), which gathers authors, TV personalities (okay, Radio 4 personalities) and commentators to discuss the meaning of literary festivals. Between them, they have written articles, collected into a book entitled *Death of Publishing and the Printed Word: Why?* (Harper-Bobbins £19.99; Also on Kindle £19.95). Don't forget to book to see David Mitchell, thinking it is the witty man off the telly when it is, in fact, the author of *Cloud Atlas*, reading

extracts from his latest work – a moving fictionalised autobi-
ography about his constant disappointment at not winning
literature's top prize: *My Booker Book* (£16.99).

Continue the self-referential discussion a week later on
London's South Bank where there will be a relentless programme of events, productions, screenings, seminars, and
workshops. The highlight is *David James*, Tom Stoppard's
moving and witty stage adaptation of David Lodge's fictional biography of Henry James. (A companion play will be
called *Henry Lodge*.) The premiere will be introduced by
former England goalkeeper David James, who will be giving his insights into post-structuralism, *Derrida and the
Death of the Author*. Meanwhile, at the Haywood Gallery, go
and see daring art installation *Literature Will Eat its Self* – in
which literary critics will be eating extracts of Will Self's
various titles printed on rice paper, some of which will be
coated with mind-altering drugs. Also, leading authors will
be staging an intervention with Douglas Coupland so they
can finally 'work out what his problem is and get him the
help he clearly needs'.

No cultural summer is complete without a visit to the
world famous *Edinburgh Fringe Festival* where you can pay
£14 to see a comedian you've never heard of; or £17 to see a
comedian you recognise from *Mock the Week* (which you, of
course, only watch ironically); or £21 for a nice-looking
three course set menu from a restaurant that Giles Coren
quite liked and is at least within sight of a theatre. There is,
of course, the *Edinburgh Military Tattoo*, but this year sees
the first *Alternative Military Tattoo*, in which ex-soldiers from
the Black Watch Third Battalion Royal Regiment draw
permanent and offensive designs on your upper thigh that
you can show off at North London dinner parties to prove
you're not boring.

You may, however, be feeling like cultural enlightenment
with a spiritual dimension. If you're in Oxford, why not join
Father Inglethorpe for his *Oxford Movement* – a delightful
walking tour taking in the sights and smells of the renowned
city's Anglo-Catholic past? Cap it with a visit to a one-man
show about a bishop considering moving to Rome with the

promise of being made a cardinal. The show is on at the Old Fire Station and is called *I Feel like a New Man*. If you understand that joke, you certainly won't be interested in a trip to Cambridge and a visit to the *White Horse Lock-Inn Experience*, in which actors recreate the clandestine conversations of Cranmer, Latimer and Tyndale discussing clerical vestments (strong ale, meat and cheese included).

But if theological controversy is your thing, and you're already getting withdrawal symptoms over Oberammergau, and have, incredibly, read this far, why not go to a little known German town in Hesse for the *Re-enactment of the Colloquy of Marburg*? Every seven years, locals dress up as Luther, Zwingli and a variety of Reformation reformers to scream at each other about the Real Presence of Christ during the Eucharist. Lots of fun, and no theological knowledge is required (bring your own bread rolls to throw).

Relax and recover at something far more ecumenical. Head over to Lourdes for 12 June and take part in a special European Whitsun service, celebrating the spiritual, international dimension of Pentecost, followed by communion with seven types of bread, conducted in fourteen languages. Book now for tickets to the *EU-charist*.

Have an enlightening summer, everyone.

The Widespread
Affliction of Biopia

or: A thinly-veiled moan about the
lack of original sitcom on TV

Until recently, you could turn on the television on any given evening, punch in a channel at random and most likely happen upon one of three types of programme – soap, reality television and detective drama. Soap actors slip into soapy medical dramas and from there into a dancing competition before becoming a deranged killer in an episode of *Lewis* or *Jonathan Creek*. It's all very reassuring during such troubled times.

But as of late, you're likely to find a fourth type of programme – biopics. The television schedules are crammed with dramas about famous people. In the last few years, we've seen biopics of Sir Winston Churchill, Sir Clive Sinclair, Mary Whitehouse, Margaret Thatcher, Tony Blair, David Blunkett to name a few. David Cameron and Boris Johnson had barely begun their political careers to find their Oxford heritage had been dramatised. Some are historically sensitive rewrites, others hysterical satirical broad swipes. You no longer even have to be dead to qualify.

Comedians have proved to be particularly rich pickings with recent biopics on Tony Hancock, Frankie Howerd, Kenneth Williams, Peter Cook and Dudley Moore, Morecambe and Wise, Hattie Jacques, the Pythons and Kenny Everett. The Goodies, meanwhile, continue to point out with a self-deprecating laugh, blended with a furious snarl, that their material isn't even repeated, let alone their lives rehashed as drama.

It is easy to understand the reason for these programmes, both to the TV commissioners and the audiences. These are low-hanging fruit that promise much juice. The private life of Mary Whitehouse can be laid bare for all to see, along with off-screen bitchings of Kenneth Williams, and the early innocence of Margaret Thatcher. These biopics all play on well-established personality 'brands'. They don't need to establish their characters because a real human being has taken the time – all of their time, in fact – to do that for us. The biopic can get on with the task of subverting, scandalising or sneering.

These programmes are not without merit. They are often very enjoyable. But they are instant. They are easily-digestible high-quality junk food; not kebabs, exactly, but one of those meals in silver dishes from M&S where you just squeeze on the lemon and put it in the oven. The results are pleasing, but deep down, you know that it's not cooking. And so with these biopics. It's interesting to imagine what Margaret Thatcher was like before she became an MP, but we all know that it was probably nothing like what we saw in the TV movie. (We should treat this with the same suspicion that we treat her own self-aggrandizing autobiographies.)

This fad speaks of a failure of the imagination. Why tell a new story about characters we've never met when we can revisit the life of Katie Price or Simon Cowell? What's the 'truth' behind these people? We know it's not real, but we want to hear something juicy. Even our fiction is derivative in this way. It is telling that one of the biggest publishing sensations of recent times was *The Da Vinci Code*. The characters are not even skin deep. They have no personality. But they find out 'the truth' about our pre-conceived and unchallenged idea of the Vatican, a truth that none of us really believes.

What nourishes us is truth. Real truth. True truth. We know we won't find it in a made-for-TV romp or in the pages of an authorised hagiography. What we look for are honest and intriguing snapshots. This is precisely what we find in the gospels – four biographies about the life of Jesus, all telling a similar tale from different stand-points. On the main points, there is close agreement, but at other points, the writers focus on very different characters and tell strikingly different stories, some strange, some hard to understand, all of them intriguing.

Let's consider the nativity. Matthew gives us magi (astrologers of all people). Luke brings us shepherds. John gives us poetic mystery. And Mark, well, he doesn't give us a sausage. At Christmas, we hear many parts of different accounts read aloud in churches, or performed by children dressed as crabs or snowflakes. But will we really hear what Matthew, Luke and John are trying to say? Or have we been worn down by the books that say that Jesus' virgin birth was probably made up by Constantine? Truth is normally stranger than fiction.

Instant Permanence

or: The pitfalls of hitting 'Send'

Writing used to be easy. More complicated in terms of typewriters, photocopiers and printers, yes. But it was reassuringly slow. The writer would write. The text or manuscript would be sent to an editor who would read, think, re-read and give thoughts. Then there would be more rewriting – possibly by hand, then more typing. Then a re-submission. Then perhaps a sub-editor would get involved. It would be typeset, printed and then eventually distributed.

All of the above would have to be accompanied by handwritten or typed letters, which slowed things down further – especially if my postal administration is anything to go by. A letter has to be thought about, suitable paper found and then written on (2–5 days). Then a corresponding envelope needs to be unearthed (2–3 days), the postal address found and written on (2–3 days), a stamp purchased (2–5 days). And then one needs to remember to post it (1–2 weeks).

This entire process was slow and expensive, so editors were fairly fussy about what got printed in the first place. But the internet has changed everything. Now, writing is instant. It probably shouldn't be, but it is. Furthermore, we are not prepared for the changes that have already taken place.

The internet throws up all kinds of contradictions and paradoxes. The Web is, theoretically, a new frontier in which content is king. It connects people with similar interests from all over the world so you can write a blog or article that runs to thousands of words, safe in the knowledge that your audience will appreciate the depth and detail. There is no editor moaning about keeping it short, or the need to leave room for adverts. And the technology itself means the Web is limitless in scope and size. Broadband enables anyone with a standard computer to download the complete works of Shakespeare, Dickens and Austen in a few seconds.

And yet the internet is no different from any other medium – it competes for your attention. Headlines, hooks, gimmicks and grabby stories still rule. Twitter is almost the embodiment of the internet. Some find the strict limitation on characters infuriating, but you can say an awful lot with just 140 characters. Plenty of sensational Bible verses are this short and can take a whole lifetime to appreciate.

But there are pitfalls here. In compressing your views on a tweet, Facebook update, message board or blog post, you may end up being crass, or say something you will regret. Even if you do think of something brilliantly concise, apt and meaningful, it still might not be a good idea to write it and send it. Some MPs, celebs and comedians have already regretted tweets and emails, where certain attitudes and prejudices have just slipped out. When writing was a slow process there was plenty of time to change your mind – days, even weeks, of a 'cooling off period'.

There's no substitute for sleeping on any written correspondence. If you write an important or tricky email, save it as a draft and come back tomorrow. Compose your blog post on a different document and transfer it later when you've had time to think. Send your communiqué to a friend, colleague or spouse first to get their opinion, especially if it's really important.

The point is that the internet is instant. You can start your own blog in moments, snap and post a picture in seconds, and post a few hundred words that can be read by anyone in the world with a computer and a phone line. One hundred years ago, the richest and most powerful person in the world did not have that kind of power. Now it just takes a smartphone.

But the immediacy of the internet is not the only pitfall. Most things in life that are instant are disposable. But not the internet. When writing online, it's best to assume that your words are more permanent than those chiselled into marble. They are there, somewhere, for *ever*. You may think you've removed the offending tweet or comment, but an imprint of your ill-advised remark will be sitting on a server somewhere in Nebraska and can be found with persistence.

Whenever I blog or tweet, I assume that any opinion I state will be thrown in my face at some point. If I apply for ordination or stand for parliament, examiners or journalists will dig around for my views on all kinds of subjects. This was particularly brought home to me when I found that some of my tweets were appearing on the back of *Broadcast* magazine and could be read by anyone who may realistically offer me work (or withdraw existing work).

In the face of this, one could be tempted to say nothing at all and be the mealy-mouthed politician who just seeks to avoid gaffes. But why blog if one is trying to avoid saying anything? What the permanence of the internet has done is force me to think carefully before writing anything, be it dashing off a blog post or tweeting.

The temptation, then, could be to blog anonymously and say what you like. Vanity stops some of us from doing that. If I say something witty, I would like to be credited. There are good reasons to avoid untraceable pen-names, like Flameguy87 or AceMavRick101. Not only do these avatars make us sound like seven-year-olds, but we can be bolstered by the liberty of anonymity. We can end up exaggerating our views, criticising people overly harshly and being hateful. Soon we find that we are in the company of gossips, slanderers and mockers because that is what we have become.

Stereotypical Comedy

or: Why it's perfectly okay to make jokes about the French

Here's a joke for you: An Englishman, an Irishman and a Scotsman go into a pub. The Englishman says something bland and conventional – or slightly stuck-up. The Scotsman in some way demonstrates he is thrifty. The Irishman demonstrates he has misunderstood the entire situation and everyone laughs at him.

Okay, so it's not a joke, but it's the format of a joke. Is it anti-Irish? I would argue not. The Irish are not an oppressed and exploited minority – any more. There would have been a time when the joke would have been inappropriate. But we're okay with it now. Aren't we? Why is that?

Jokes and comedy often rely on stereotypes, not because the joke writer is lazy or prejudiced, necessarily, but because they are short-cuts. Sometimes they're clichéd, sometimes very current. Sometimes they are sweepingly generalised, and other times they are specific. But the format is clear.

Jokes require a number of things in order to work. A key one is surprise. But in order to surprise, you need to establish 'the normal' as quickly as possible in order to subvert it. It's why, in this land of jokes, cabbies tend to be racist and tell you who they had in the back of their cab the other day, builders work slowly and have four sugars in their tea, estate agents are liars, teenagers don't speak, air stewardesses wear heavy make-up, and blondes are stupid.

In the same way, when someone starts to tell a David Beckham joke, you know that it's a generic joke about stupid person. And it has been assumed David Beckham is stupid. I'm not sure he is. He is softly spoken and has a fairly high-pitched voice, which makes him sound slightly comical. But it doesn't make him stupid. I note that he's considerably richer than everyone who reads this book combined so he's not that stupid. But because he's a multi-millionaire with a pop star wife who doesn't take himself very seriously, no one feels that sorry for him. It's probably okay. But we'll come back to this.

Here's a standard European joke:

In Heaven, the mechanics are German, the chefs are French, the police are British, the lovers are Italian and everything is organised by the Swiss. In Hell, the mechanics are French, the police are German, the chefs are British, the lovers are Swiss and everything is organised by the Italians. (*EU Book of Humour Vol III Page 321 Paragraph 2b – Ratified 2003 pending Cultural Subcommittee approval*)

It seems harmless enough. What's the joke? There are several and all based around stereotypes. The Germans are good with machines but officious, the British are fairminded, but poor cooks, the Swiss are organised but unromantic and the Italians make great lovers but are, by and large, a shambles. These stereotypes are broadly accepted as being true. They must be true enough for the joke to be funny otherwise the joke wouldn't work. Which it does. There are undoubtedly notable exceptions to the stereotypes, but no one's too concerned because poms/limeys/roastbeefs, wops, dagoes, krauts, frogs and, er, the Swiss are all of similar status.

Some say it's not okay to joke about nationalities and stereotype in this way or any way. They seem to think there is some sort of EU/UN standard to joke-telling, saying 'Why is it okay to joke about Americans when it's not okay to joke about Nigerians?' We all know that this issue is complicated, but there is a way through. It is okay to make jokes about Americans and the French. And, if you're British, there's a good reason not to make jokes about Nigerians, as we shall see.

No one really knows how comedy works. There's not a 'Grand Unified Theory' of comedy that I've found convincing, or a 'Standard Model', but in this area of joking about 'people groups' and all that, I think there are three categories of joke.

Category 1: A Joke told between Equals.

This is essentially banter between colleagues, brothers and friends – about each other and not designed to cause offence. If anything, it comes from a place of respect and affection, based on the fact that there is general equality, e.g. jokes about the French by the English – and vice versa. Let's be honest. The French and the English are not all that different. We've had a bumpy relationship over the last thousand years, but for the last hundred years at least, we've been on the same side. We're both large, industrious, wealthy countries with nuclear weapons and we're not afraid of each other. A joke about the French obsession with food or lack of personal hygiene is probably fine. It's worth watching *Flushed Away*. There is a French character – a Frog! Who'd have thought it? – voiced by Jean Reno. There are some very funny jokes at the expense of the French, but they're clearly not meant to wound.

But there would be circumstances in which anti-French jokes would be unethical and unacceptable. Imagine you're in a class of English teenagers and there is one solitary French exchange student in your midst for a week or two. The English teenagers tell a relentless series of jokes again and again at the expense of the French student – based on crude national stereotypes. Is that appropriate? Almost certainly not.

Category 2: A Joke told by the Righteous Weak against the Unrighteous Powerful.

In this type of joke, we're veering towards satire. Here we have, for example, jokes by left-wing broke students against a right-wing government. Some of these jokes will be justified – others less so, depending on your politics. David Cameron, as Prime Minister and an old Etonian, and therefore powerful and privileged, is fair game. No one's going to feel too sorry for him on this front because he's had things his own way for most of his life.

That said, he's suffered tragedy recently with the loss of his six-year-old son who suffered from cerebral palsy and a form of epilepsy. None of this has anything to do with his politics, wealth or status. It's hard to see how a joke about the death of his son could ever be justified comedically or even satirically. You are certainly unlikely to carry an audience with you on that one.

We encounter problems here because this sort of comedy, against the powerful, will delight the less powerful and offend the friends of the powerful. Moreover, comedy of this nature, satire in particular, is intended to offend. It's exposing hypocrisy or cold-heartedness or other vices. Those affected or mocked will be offended by the accusations. And all of this is why, ultimately, offence is a very poor indicator of whether a joke should have been told or not.

3. A Joke told by the Powerful against the Powerless.

This is comedy used to humiliate, oppress and marginalise. This is why it's inappropriate for an Englishman to tell Pakistani jokes – even though there are 160 million Pakistanis in Pakistan and they have nuclear weapons. They are a powerful nation, but in Britain they are a minority and frequently get a rough deal from those who are simply racist. It would be irresponsible to make jokes about Pakistanis, perhaps even valid satirical ones, if we were increasing injustice against them and their overall suffering as a minority.

Jokes can be told about a minority by members of that minority. Is it okay to tell a string of Jewish jokes? If you're Jackie Mason on a West End stage, yes. The jokes are told from within a community with affection. If you're a skinhead and leading a fascist rally, no. The jokes are being told to humiliate, oppress and encourage hatred. There is obviously a difference. This is because it matters who is telling the joke, and who is listening.

There is an added complication, however. It comes when the person telling the joke is a fictional character, especially one who is either confused or unsympathetic. An obvious example would be Alf Garnett. (For our American readers, that would be Archie Bunker.) We are not being invited to agree with his views. The tricky bit is when stand-up comedians do this kind of material and are assuming that we are assuming that they can't possibly mean what they're saying. This seems morally murky.

The fact is every joke takes place within a context – socially and dramatically, and it can make the world of difference what the context is. Some of this stuff is really hard to figure out, e.g. animated characters get to be much more visceral and offensive than live action characters (see *South Park* and *Family Guy*). But whether we should prevent people from saying things we think are beyond the pale and simply too offensive is a separate question.

So that's a simplified but still over-technical explanation about why certain jokes can cause offence but are still basically okay, even if they are a little tired or predictable at times. Which means I can tell you this really funny joke about a Frenchman, cycling along when the string of onions falls off from around his neck and … no? Oh.

Coming to a Small Screen Near You

or: More jokes, this time at the expense of British television

Summer brings with it many things – undercooked barbe-cued chicken, the discovery of sand in every piece of cloth-ing (including clothes you didn't even wear that day on the beach) and TV schedules that smack of defeat. No matter how many times the publicity material says 'another chance to see …' we all know it's a repeat. But fret not. Exciting new programmes are just around the corner.

This September, look out for BBC1's brand new sit-com *My Stepmother is Galadriel*. Widower Seymour has his life turned upside down when he falls in love with the Queen of the Elves who is washed up on the beach. Galadriel had been hoping to sail to the West, not to be shipwrecked in Weston-Super-Mare! Uh-oh. Soon she's about to realise that the land of humans is not as simple as she once thought …

But if drama is your bag, look no further. See ex-soapstars play only slightly different roles from their previous part in these fabulous new shows. BBC1's *Coppers* is a gritty police drama about the lives and loves of six police officers in Dover. One of them is Irish, so that'll be funny. Alternatively, BBC2's *On the Beat* is a gritty police drama about the lives and loves of seven police offices on the beat in Newcastle. One of them is Welsh and an absolute scream. And three are women. ITV has two cop shows coming. One takes us back to the 1930s and into a small, quirky town in the Scottish

Highlands as Englishman PC James Webster has to win the trust of the quirky locals, find missing sheep and deal with the mayor's daughter who just won't take no for an answer. A heart-warming, quirky comedy drama for Sunday nights. Midweek, *Maxwell* is a gritty police drama about the life and loves of a fifty-something divorced police detective with issues. Set in Manchester. And don't forget to set the video for Channel 4's *Boys in Blue* – a gritty police drama about the lives and loves of five police officers in London's Tower Hamlets. And there's always Channel 5's *Detroit Nights* – a gritty police drama about the lives and loves of five police officers in a tough city.

Also, look out for amateur sleuth, *Michelle* – a stripper-gram who goes round Bristol strutting her stuff and solving murders that have been inexplicably passed over by the police. We suspect foul play, but it turns out the policemen just aren't very good at their jobs but they do make amusing innuendos about Michelle's figure.

If you prefer your movies, watch *Hollywood Puff*. Catch all that latest movie news, interviews, previews and reviews. Plus, there's *'The Making of' Hollywood Puff* which looks at how TV channels can legally show shameless thirty minute movie promos and why the young, attractive host has to contractually laugh at the jokes of film stars in interviews and not refer to some serious turkeys they've starred in before. Also, see how a pre-allocated four-minute interview with a film-star is made to look like a proper, substantial interview before they're hustled out so the *TV Quick* movie correspondent can have ninety seconds with Brendan Fraser, just so she can tell her friends she met him. This all explains why every film is recommended regardless, even if it stars Jean-Claude Van Damme.

If you like to keep things real, a new raft of reality TV programmes is floating your way. *At Your Convenience* is a fly-on-the-wall documentary following six toilet attendants in London's West End. One of them is really mean and bitchy, but it's okay because he's quite camp as well.

Daytime TV revamps the daily talk show with *Trasha* – People who've married too near on the family tree shout at each other in front of an audience. After all, where better to sort out family problems than in a multi-camera studio in front of strangers on national television?

Seriously Awkward – Documentary series looking at couples who've discovered that sorting out family problems on national television isn't ideal for long-term success.

Who's Laughing Now? – Series looking at washed-up comedians who are annoyingly content at being out of the media spotlight after their fifteen minutes of fame ran out, including seven past winners of *Opportunity Knocks*, and that bloke called Duncan something-or-other who said 'Chase me'.

Plus C4's reality archaeology game-show *Show me the Mummy* in which teams led by Tony Robinson and Ann Widdecombe solve clues and plunder as many genuine ancient tombs as possible in an hour.

Don't be worried about dumbing down. Why not be one of an elite 3000 to regularly watch Germaine Greer host BBC4's entertainment review *I Preferred the Book*? Feel smugly superior as *Captain Corelli, About a Boy* and other films get systematically slated for changed endings, erased characters and plot-twists that just seem completely unnecessary? Even *The English Patient* is cautioned for emphasising the wrong relationship.

And never let it be said that the religious are chronically underserved by television. Look out for *Good Heavens!* - Michaela Strachan talks to the Bishop of Norwich and narrowly avoids talking about Jesus, before he chooses his favourite Bing Crosby records. Meanwhile, John Craven walks around graveyards and wonders if we've got room to bury everyone.

There Should Be A City Here – John McCarthy trails round the Middle East wondering whether anything in the Bible could have actually happened. Apparently it couldn't have done.

Creed – Richard Dawkins, Elaine Storkey and a lady from the *Guardian* talk about why there's suffering. You've seen them do it on TV hundreds of times before, but this time, they're pretty sure they'll come up with the answer.

One to miss: *The Richards*. Channel 4's reality documentary in the household of pop-legend Cliff Richard, because, let's face it, he can't be like that all the time. Turns out he is. Boring. Plus there's only one guy called Richard, so technically it should be *The Richard* and that's not his real name anyway.

Happy viewing!

Part Two:
The Economy, the
Banks and all
things Financial

*'Among the rich you will never
find a really generous man even
by accident. They may give their
money away, but they will never
give themselves away ... To be
smart enough to get all that
money you must be dull enough
to want it.'*

G.K. Chesterton

Since we're getting on so well, it seems a shame to bring things to a screeching halt by discussing politics, so let us postpone the inevitable and let us next turn to the subject of our wallets.

We Brits are pretty odd about money on the whole. But we tend to agree about money when we're talking other people's. The prevailing view of our time is that the rich seem to have too much money and that the poor don't have enough. To break it down further into categories we have the 'super-rich' as well as 'well-off'. And there are two types of poor: the 'deserving' and the 'undeserving'.

What we do to address these inequalities is, of course, a political, moral and ethical problem, so our discussion of politics is closer than we might think. But for now, let us take the deeply embarrassing subject of money. What follows is a collection of chapters including ones about Mortgages, Money, Banks and Brunel. But let us begin with the scintillating subject of taxation.

Haves and Have-Nots, Part 1: The Robin Hood Tax

or: How I've ended up on the side of the Sheriff of Nottingham

BBC Radio 4 broadcasts a fine comedy programme called *Mark Thomas: The Manifesto*, in which members of his audience suggest policies for a political manifesto that would make Britain a better place. It's funny and inventive. After all, we all have our pet peeves that we would like to see banned by parliament – like caravans, cravats or Piers Morgan. Mark Thomas taps into the fact that passing laws has become something of a national obsession. There now exists a catalogue of laws which essentially amount to 'Hey, you lot. Play nicely' and 'Don't make me come down there.' Thomas would naturally approve since he's a socialist, and to the socialist, everyone's business is the government's business.

Socialists – and plenty of others – do this because they feel the markets don't help the poor. They are convinced they are right about this. Because they are. The market has an invisible hand – which is also a cold one. But the State has two hands which are equally icy – law and taxation. In fact, calling them hands implies a certain degree of subtlety is possible with them, but law and tax are, in fact, heavy blunt instruments.

Now I take it as a given that we *all* want to help the poor – Christians and non-Christians; socialists and libertarians.

The Left's accusations that those on the Right have no regard for the poor is extremely lazy and disingenuous. Those on the Right believe the State is either ill-placed or unauthorised to help the poor. Sure, some on the Right don't care about the poor because they're mean. But some of the Left don't care about the poor either – they just want to see the rich impoverished. Neither the Right nor the Left has the monopoly on virtue.

The problem with being on the Right, then, is perpetually trying to put one's point across without sounding mean. Therefore opposing this 'magic wand' tax, The Robin Hood Tax, puts me against the likes of Oxfam, Barnardo's, Action-Aid, the Salvation Army and the TUC (although I obviously don't mind opposing that last one) and, mostly worryingly me for me, Richard Curtis.

So it would appear that, by default, I am on the side of the Sheriff of Nottingham. The irony is, of course, that historically the Sheriff was the one imposing too many taxes and that Robin Hood was rebelling *against* taxation, so historically, I'm actually the one with Robin Hood. But that is not how it plays in the popular media.

Why the Word 'Progressive' is Profoundly Annoying

Robin Hood seems to be everywhere at the moment. There was the recent Saturday teatime BBC TV series. Then Russell Crowe gave us his Robin Hood. (Some of us wanted to give it back.) And on Radio 4 recently, Matthew Parris played host to Clive Stafford Smith on *Great Lives*. Our favourite human rights lawyer was arguing Robin Hood's corner, revealing a life-long passion for the character. Whilst freely admitting that no such person existed, he said that Robin Hood was essentially a 'progressive'. The word 'progressive' came up a few times. And I've been hearing that word non-stop ever since.

When a coalition government was being formed, there was much talk about a 'progressive' alliance between Labour and the Liberal democrats. The word was bandied around frequently, but never examined or challenged. What is it to be 'progressive' in the political sense? One could be rather cynical like *The Times'* Daniel Finkelstein, who says '*Progressive* is the sort of word that communists used to use in the 1980s when they were organising conferences that they didn't want you to know were financed by the Soviet Union.' But then he would say that, wouldn't he?

Putting one's coat on the term progressive is a very clever move. Firstly, it renders all opponents 'regressive' or, at best, 'static'. In one sense they're right, since their opponents are called 'Conservatives' who presumably want things to stay as they are, or go back to being how they were. To some, that is a good thing. But many who lived through the misery of the 1970s don't want to go back there, even though many of the woes were caused by 'progressive' policies. In fact, in the early 1980s, the ones who were advocating radical change – or progress – were the Thatcherites. No one has ever accused them of being progressive.

This is why the word 'progressive' is so powerful since it gives the impression that one wants to move forward to a new dawn and a brighter day in a positive, upbeat way without giving any indication of how that is going to be achieved and at what cost. It doesn't even say specifically what we are 'progressing' towards. Like all political wonks, the progressives like to talk in abstract nouns like 'justice' and 'fairness' – again, who could argue with those? – but the mundane reality about progressive politics is that it's a general belief in taxing rich people and giving the money to the poor people.

On the surface, this seems like an excellent idea. What's not to like? We don't like people being poor and we like the idea of giving them money. We don't like rich people and they have money so we should take money from the high and mighty and give it to the cheeky chirpy poor. Just like Robin Hood did.

Except we should probably note that Robin Hood legendarily '*stole* from the rich to give to the poor'. What he legendarily did was illegal and unconstitutional. In one sense, then, it's a good name for the tax, since it exposes it for what it is – a dodgy plundering of the rich for the sake of the poor. Its heart is surely in the right place, but its head is firmly in the sand.

Now we could ask the 'What would Jesus do?' question here. After all, Robin Hood is all about helping the poor and social justice and so in that way seems to be a Jesus-type. What's more, Jesus warned about the dangers of wealth as much as anything else. He told stories of corpulent fat-cats who tore down their barns to build bigger ones, not realising that they wouldn't even make it through the night alive.

But Jesus advocated that the wealthy give their riches away voluntarily. He doesn't suggest the mob turn up to Zaccheus' house and help themselves – or even rob the rich Zaccheus in order to give his money to the poor. But this is effectively what 'progressive' rates of taxation are, except the mob has voted for it, and this time turn up in a nice-looking police uniforms if you don't co-operate.

Moreover, Zaccheus gained much of his wealth illegitimately and was rightly ashamed of himself. But it seems now that *all* wealth is suspicious. There is a sense that anyone who is rich must have gotten that money by lying, cheating, mis-selling or making someone else poor. And therefore the progressive line is that the only moral thing to do is take that money away and give it to someone poor so that everyone can feel better. This view of wealth is not a biblical one. Money is shown to be dangerous but not, in itself, bad. In fact, for Abraham, Job and Solomon, it was a sign of divine blessing.

At one point in the radio interview, Mr Stafford Smith began singing the theme tune to the old Robin Hood song (where he's riding through the glen). Matthew Parris joined in. It was dreadful, but enlightening at the point where Matthew Parris correctly sang 'feared by the bad'. Mr Stafford Smith sang, without thinking, 'feared by the rich'. It was an interesting and revealing subconscious slip – but it's one that many people all over Britain have already made.

Who's Going to Notice £250 Billion?

But the clever thing about the Robin Hood Tax is that it does not appear unjust or onerous, but a mere trifle. The publicity material is at pains to point out that only a tiny, tiny, tiny percentage of every speculative bank to bank transaction would be taken. Just five pence for every thousand pounds. Who's going to notice that? And then they brag that it should raise at least £250 billion a year annually. Now even the most talentless of bankers would notice that amount of money missing. That'll definitely eat into their bonuses.

And then they'll make everyone else pay. That's what bankers do. It's one of the main reasons why people don't like them – because they are really good at making the people pay. As a result of a Robin Hood Tax, the cost of the transactions would go up, and so fees would go up, lending rates would be a little higher, industry and retail would pay the price and everything in the shops gets a little more expensive – so again, the burden of taxation falls on the poor, who are always the most heavily taxed whilst already being tied up by bureaucracy and form-filling for welfare programmes.

Bill Nighy, who starred in the advertising campaign, told BBC Radio 5 Live: 'The banks should ... make good the damage caused by the economic crisis but should also perpetually become a useful thing in society.' Banks do actually create wealth. They probably create less than they claim, but they do actually create wealth rather than just print it like Gordon Brown, David Cameron and Robert Mugabe do. Out of those three men, only Robert Mugabe is the one honest enough not to re-label it 'quantitative easing'. The banks are part of the nation's wealth creation, which the state then lavishly spends, whilst asking us to be grateful.

Anyway, Mr Nighy, you and I both work in the media. We should be fairly cautious about telling people who is and who is not socially 'useless'.

Homes and Castles, Part 1: Mortgages

or: How and why I went right off my bank

Life is full of rites of passage. When I meet a new dad, a yawning wreck with chapped hands from all that hand-washing, I give a knowing look and a smile of recognition. Okay, I'll be honest, it borders on smugness.

But I'm on the receiving end at the moment since I'm applying for a mortgage. Get the smiling out of the way. Wipe that smug grin off your face. I've saved all the money I've made from writing over the last ten years and am buying a door knocker for a new house. All I need to do now is find the money to buy the rest of the property. Hence, I need a mortgage.

It might be pushing it to make further comparisons between applying for a mortgage and childbirth. There are lots of leaflets involved. And if you're a freelancer, it's about the same level of humiliation. You go into a dull windowless room and lay yourself bare, showing your paperwork and life choices to a total stranger, to be poked and prodded, although in this case screaming is frowned upon.

At first, I had naively hoped that this sorry situation could have been avoided. After all, *my* bank knows me. I've been with them for nearly thirty years (since the age of about seven, in fact). My bank has had a front row seat to my tedious, financially uncomplicated but mostly solvent life, witnessing virtually every transaction I have ever made. In view of this, coupled with the number of pieces of glossy paper they've sent me over the years saying how important I am to them, I thought we had a relationship. But I was mistaken.

They send me bland, forgettable letters whispering that they're dropping the interest rate of my saver account to 0.1% for no obvious reason. They send me frightening letters in Times New Roman to tell me one of my accounts is slightly overdrawn. They can't phone me to tell me this so I can avoid a £25 charge. That's just not possible, apparently. I believed them until the moment I was paid a large sum of money at which point I got a call asking me if I'd like them to invest it for me.

I must have been taken in by their adverts in which they claim that banking with them is lovely. They're lovely. I'm lovely. And we can all be lovely in an animated pastel-coloured, big-eyed world of loveliness.

All of this covered up that the reality that high-street banking has been utterly dehumanised. You haven't been able to pop in and see your bank manager for years. We abandoned being able to talk to someone who is in charge of our life savings, credit cards and direct debits long ago. Instead, we aspire to a meaningful relationship with our butcher so we can be sure of the provenance of the meat we eat. This doesn't seem right, somehow.

The trouble is that we have made our own trade-off between 'paid for' and 'free'. We Brits love a bargain. And we like free. It's easily the most popular price-point. But the Executive Director of the Bank of England has said that banking should not be free. It's beautiful that it is a banker who is telling us we should be paying banks more money for their services. And it's an even greater irony that he's probably right. But don't worry. No one will listen to him. We have had free banking for so long, the idea of paying to bank is an anathema.

In truth, I might be able to pay extra for a customer relationship manager, but this won't buy me a relationship. I've been offered various accounts at my bank named after precious metals, but these don't seem to offer much: more travel insurance than I'll ever need and insufficient AA cover. I still won't be able to call up a manager that I will ever meet. This customer relationship manager, as the title suggests, manages the *relationship* – not you. Or the bank. They don't have any power or influence. They can't lend you any of the bank's money. They have to get you to fill in forms so that they can fill in forms so that some boffins can put the figures into a spreadsheet and pass it through an algorithm designed by even cleverer boffins – the type that designed the Credit Default Swap.

And so every time we expect our bank to do something helpful like phone us up when we're about to go into the red, or even think about giving us a mortgage, we relearn the lesson: the market has a very cold hand. But we don't want to be in the icy grip of capitalism. We want the warm handshake of a bank manager who knows us and trusts us. But these things require the greatest long-term investments that we're never quite prepared to make – trust and time.

The Theory of Money, Part 1: Making Money

or: What's my motivation?

A short while ago, I was in the office of a BBC executive producer. I can't remember why. Perhaps it was celebrating a sitcom I've been developing coming up for its second birthday without yet having actually been offered to any of the BBC channels. I suggested we offer the show to BBC4, but was told that their budgets were too small, and that in any case, BBC4 was no longer allowed to make comedy. This new unbreakable policy, like most BBC new unbreakable policies, was reversed within a few months.

I pointed out that so far, BBC4 hadn't really failed with a comedy. Its strike rate is almost 100 per cent, birthing *Lead Balloon*, *The Thick of It*, *Getting On* and the much overlooked gem, *The Great Outdoors*. When the question was asked about why a low-budget, documentary-based backwater has the best sitcom success rate in British television, I ventured an answer. I said it was *because* the shows were low budget. These weren't making anyone rich, so the people making them were doing it for love, or the craft, not the money. My theory fell on deaf ears. I went on to say that most people, especially writers, are not motivated by money. They just want to do good work and make a living.

The executive producer laughed out loud at this. She said she had been dragged in to numerous negotiations over fees and payments and contracts. From where she was sitting, it seemed it was *mostly* about the money. I can see how it would seem so from her position. But that is the problem with BBC and all large institutions: the contract is everything. The contract exists because ultimately there is no presumption of goodwill. It must all be written down. And once this happens, suddenly it's about the money.

I stand by my theory. All the writers I know are not motivated by money. Money is just one of the things they need so that they can write, which is what they live to do.

Barely anyone is motivated by money itself, anyway. Those who only want money are usually consumed by it. Take Hetty Green, the New York millionaire, who refused a hernia operation in her old age because it cost $150, when she herself was worth over $100 million. This is a hundred years ago so that's billions in today's money. But these bizarre stories of frugality-as-lunacy are rare.

It is true that 'the love of money is the root of all kinds of evil'. But the money is not normally wanted in itself. People seek money for all kinds of reasons; to gain freedom from worry; or to prove their worth to their old school friends; or to show that they are winning. Investor Warren Buffett is worth nearly $50 billion, and yet lives in the same house he bought in 1958 for $31,500. He seems comparatively un-interested in leading the lifestyle of the multi-billionaire. It would appear the money is a way of demonstrating that as far as investments go, he was right all along.

It is an irony that the companies that seek to make money, above all else, often fail. That is the argument of John Kay in his interesting (but annoyingly inconsistent) book, *Obliquity*. He says that ICI started having problems when key scientists left the company when it kept emphasising short-term profit over long-term research. It's easy to see that from ICI's mission statement from 1991 which causes both anger and drowsiness at the same time. Here it is:

'The ICI Group's vision is to be the industry leader in creative value for customers and shareholders through market leadership, technological edge and a world competitive cost-base.'

Translation: 'We want to be the best at saving our customers money whilst making our shareholders as much money as possible by spending as little as possible on training and technology whilst screwing down our suppliers – in the area of work that, you know, ICI does. Whatever it is that we make. Is it fertilizer? I forget. Whatever's most profitable, I guess.' Truly inspiring.

The big banks came unstuck because they tried to turn money into more money merely by shifting it around, repackaging it, swapping it with someone else's, before insuring the whole thing and then wondering where their money went when the market turned. The government tried solving the problem by merely speaking money into existence and calling it 'quantitative easing'. But in our heart of hearts, we know that money doesn't work like that. Money is a bi-product of services or manufacturing or creativity, not something to be made for its own sake.

I know this is true, because you should see what I get paid for writing this book. Good job I'm not in this for the money. But then, who is?

Rest and Retirement, Part 1: Retirement

or: The marching grey doom

Plenty of apocalypses have been promised in recent years. In the 1970s, there was the possibility of all-out nuclear Armageddon. (There still is, but fortunately India and Pakistan regularly play cricket against each to let off steam.) When the Soviet Union collapsed, and we crawled out of our bunkers blinking in the bright lights, we terrified ourselves with stories of even brighter lights from alien invaders. Then it was earth-shattering meteors that would wipe out the planet's entire population. Then 9/11 happened and it was holy wars between radical Islam and the West. By the time we'd got used to that, and we all felt flush with cash and ever-rising house prices, we had the luxury of being terrified by ever-rising sea-levels. And then the money ran out.

In fact, the money had run out several years earlier although financial reality is not something our government worried about in the years before the global financial meltdown. Hardly anyone batted an eyelid at the promises about pensions made to over 6 million public sector employees and all future pensioners, not least because the promises seemed nothing out of the ordinary compared to the hopelessly ill-conceived financial planning of the past. In fact, if anything, they seemed a little mean.

Back in the good old days, the state could make grand, hubristic 'cradle-to-grave' promises because the populous could be relied upon to do the decent thing and work on a diet of mostly fried food and twenty cigarettes a day until the age of 65 before retiring with very low expectations, and dying in their early 70s of something untreatable.

But the promises kept coming, even as recently as 2006 when our Prime Minister Gordon Brown (remember him?) used his talent at spending huge amounts of money that never existed by increasing key public sector workers' pensions by 20 per cent over a couple of years. Now, the official figures put our state pension liability at £1.4 trillion, and public sector pension commitments at £800 billion. So, the government owes its private and public pensioners £2.2 trillion – for which you could gold plate an area the size of Wales. This is the real apocalypse for the nation.

The idiocy of this sort of behaviour is hard to comprehend. Many people alive today will, most likely, live into their 90s, dying of something untreatable, but delayable at great expense. Moreover, they'll look for a way of retiring at 55 if at all possible.

Unless George Osbourne manages to win Switzerland in a game of cards, this entire area will need root and branch reform. But the prevailing wisdom seems to be that because wild unaffordable promises have been made to previous generations, they have to be made to future ones. It's only fair. The latest initiative has been the raising of the retirement age by a single year, which is like pouring the contents of a kettle on a coming glacier. The crushing doom continues to advance.

It's worth noting that the idea of retirement has rather crept up on us – or at least changed over the years. When life expectancy was lower, people retired because they were too elderly to work and needed financial provision. As healthcare and diet improved, retirement became a short period of enjoying yourself before the onset of old age. Now retirement seems to be a period in which the older generation can let their hair down before it disappears, see the world, acquire new skills, drink good wine, get a sun tan and do some voluntary work.

It is, of course, anyone's right to pack in work whenever they like and spend their hard earned money on whatever they want. But there is a widespread perception that idea that employment is something you do until you are 'let off' and allowed to have a lovely long leisure-filled retirement. This implies that work is bad, or for suckers, or not what we were created to do. But work is good. It's what we were made by the Creator to do. People often think that the Garden of Eden was a work-free paradise – like a Center Parcs with better, cheaper food – and that Adam and Eve's work was a punishment for eating the forbidden fruit. But Genesis 2:15 does not say 'The LORD God put man in the Garden of Eden to work it and take care of it until he could plausibly get someone else to do it for less money while he went cruising up the Euphrates.' The Bible doesn't really have a category for retirement.

The huge liabilities of the state still need to be paid for. The obvious solution is to raise the age of retirement to something more in line with life expectancy – like 75 or more. Come on! We could do that. Let's brazen out the riots which will, at least, be quiet, orderly and leave very little litter. It will also have no impact on the news agenda, as it will happen before most of the media have made it out of bed. The pensioners will be marching around Parliament Square at 6am in order to 'beat the traffic' while the hacks are still stumbling out of bed listening to *Farming Today*.

Besides, I'm still trying to figure out how to do my job (as this book proves). By the age of 66, I might have a clue as to what I'm doing. Who knows? By 2041, my writing might start to make sense, be well argued *and* funny. That would be a start.

The Theory of Money, Part 2: Capitalism

or: How to organise a really good famine

There is a worrying trend afoot. A small minority with a strong agenda have hijacked our schools, our politicians and our media with a dogma that flies in the face of all reason, scientific research and evidence that stretches back for thousands of years. They want capitalism to be thought of as a theory, not a historical fact.

Since the collapse of numerous banks in the last few years, journalists and commentators have been talking about the End of Capitalism. Without laughing. This seems odd. Please don't misunderstand me. I really do come to bury the Lehmann Brothers, not to praise them. The utter idiocy of the bankers, the analysts, the fund-managers, the regulators and the governments is beyond question. In the plethora of documentaries and features on the great crash, lots of very wealthy people wearing suits worth more than my car said they could not have predicted this economic perfect storm.

Really? Hundreds of millions of dollars were lent to millions of barely numerate poor people who were deceived by mortgage brokers into buying a house that anyone could see they couldn't really afford. These mortgages were all bundled up, sold on, packaged and bundled, insured and sold again. What on earth did they think was going to happen when the discount mortgage rates ended? It's like giving a machine gun to a child, putting blanks in the first magazine, but live ammo in the rest, and scratching your head at the state of the playroom after a few hours.

I do not defend professional dunderheadedness on this scale. But neither do I say that Capitalism is Ending, when it simply isn't the case. And furthermore, it cannot ever be the case. Capitalism is not a theory, propounded by the evil Adam Smith. It is a fact. Allow me to explain.

Capitalism is, in one sense, an arrangement. It is the decision by a people-group to allow trade and industry to be run by private citizens and corporations rather than by the state. If a country loses its mind, it can allow all trade and industry to be run by the state. This normally happens by a small minority using force (see History of Russia, China, Cuba, etc.) since communism is such a palpably terrible idea no one would vote for it. Or least, once they'd seen it in action no one would continue to vote for it. But a little force goes a long way when coupled with brassy promises to the proletariat that have no prospect of being honoured. (See History of Russia, China, Cuba, etc.)

The state then sets about trying to run everything while the citizens get on trying to circumvent the System, or join the Party and get special privileges. Why? We know it's a human right to buy and sell good and services, not the preserve of the state. Capitalism is not just a system but a fact.

We may like to think that some societies have been untouched by capitalism – or if anything, impoverished by Western capitalism. And yet in those societies we find locals haggling in markets over goats and oats. Should they be unfortunate enough to devolve this task to the state, they will probably, at some point, starve. Serious long-term famines are almost always caused by governments, not the weather. Take a look at Chinese and Russian history in the last hundred years to find some really glaring examples.

This is not to say that capitalism is good. Capitalism can be good. Like gravity. Gravity ensures that your loved ones and possessions don't simply float off into the air. But capitalism and gravity can both be painful if you're in the wrong place at the wrong time. But it doesn't make either of them morally defective. It's what you do with them that counts.

The claim that capitalism is always a force for good is, however, not true. Capitalism, like gravity, has to be used morally and ethically. If you use capitalism to legally line your own pockets while taking the shirt off a man's back, you've done a bad thing. It doesn't make you a criminal. It makes you a jerk. You can't pin your cruel, selfish intentions on a faceless concept like capitalism – just as you can't push someone out of a third floor window, shrug and claim they were killed by gravity. But preaching that the Credit Crunch spelled the end of capitalism is like giving gravity an expiry date. It's madness and frequently ends in hunger. We must resist.

Homes and Castles, Part 2: New Homes

or: A new kind of Nimbyism

Nothing seems to delight a TV controller more than a programme that attempts a lengthy futile quest to arrange people or concepts in some sort of order of merit, like *Top 100 Recipes in the World Ever* or *10 Highest Grossing Movie Flops.*

One of the better series of this kind was the quest to find the Greatest Briton about ten years ago. It threw up some pleasing anomalies. One was a curiously high listing for Michael Crawford. Another was a surprisingly superb documentary by Jeremy Clarkson. Say what you like about the man, his politics, his face, his hair, his jeans, his TV friends, and his Chipping Camden neighbours, his documentary on Isambard Kingdom Brunel was stunning. It was passionate, informative and reverent about the man's extraordinary ability to think big, design creatively, engineer cleverly and build to the highest specifications. Brunel was truly a master at spending other people's money.

The documentary catapulted Brunel to a podium position in the Great Briton poll and made an ungrateful nation realise that his legacy was so immense that we had taken it for granted and run it into the ground years ago. I would argue that it was Clarkson's documentary and Brunel's high placing in that poll that enabled Danny Boyle to cast Kenneth Branagh to play the high-hatted engineer at the London Olympics Opening Ceremony.

It is a sad irony that a nation that led the world in industrialisation and infrastructure should have allowed it to crumble. Our rusty rail network is bursting at the seams as commuters try to avoid clogging up roads with their cars. Another irony is that highly sophisticated workshops in the south of England design state-of-the-art car parts for super-cars, but everyone knows that the 7 litre, high-performance vehicle will still only do 15mph crawling up the Fulham Palace Road towards Hammersmith.

Any talk of high-speed connections, super-fast rail links and new motorways seem fantastical, not because of the lack of British technology. This country makes buses, trams and train carriages that are exported all over the world. It's not even the eye-watering cost, but mainly because of Nimbyism.

We Britons are a curious bunch. We are a nation that will celebrate an embittered old lady refusing to sell her house to a large corporation and insisting motorway lanes go either side of her cottage and vegetable patch. And it is the same with building houses. As I have written in another chapter, I railed against my now-ex-bank and their decision not lend me a meaningful amount of money because I have been attempting to purchase a house.

Until 2012, I was a resident of Fulham, renting a house and unable to purchase any kind of habitable property in the locality because Russian Oligarchs and French Bankers keep spending seven-figure sums on houses in the area. There simply aren't enough houses to go round and the market has decided that it is much more sensible that local houses be sold to those making millions from natural resources in other countries or those seeking to avoid high taxes in France. The market is an ass. An efficient ass, but an ass nonetheless.

In fact, it was for family rather than financial reasons, we decided to leave London and now live in the lush meadows and verdant pastures of Somerset. Or at least, we are renting a house on a large housing estate near some lush meadows while someone else turns a verdant pasture a few miles away into seven houses, of which we are purchasing one. It commands spectacular views of fields, meadows, pastures and paddocks. For now.

Soon after the sale was agreed, offers accepted, mortgages offered and properties surveyed, the local newspaper informed us that a local developer was exploring an 800 home development on the fields, meadows, pastures and paddocks near my new house.

My frustration with this situation is borne from the fact that my opposition to this proposal is entirely selfish and personal. One can raise objections easily enough. Those fields are a flood plain but they must know that. The traffic in the town is already heavily congested (but is nothing like as bad as the aforementioned Fulham Palace Road which is, I am sure, one of the slowest roads in the Northern Hemisphere.) And I'm not sure where all the residents of these new homes are going to work.

But ultimately, my only real problem with these proposed houses is that they won't look very nice from my patio. I'm not a NIMBY. I'm a DRAVOLIDO – Don't Ruin the Amazing View Of Land I Don't Own. If I'm honest, that is the only real basis for my complaint.

The whole issue has, however, made me glad I'm a Christian. I have no real control over who builds what where. And the so-called democratic planning processes in this seem rather opaque and the developer is extremely well-connected. This could be crushing. After all, if this life is the only one we get, we'll furiously defend our domestic idyll with a pitchfork. But this building we're buying may be my house for twenty years, or forty years or more. Who knows? But it won't be my true home. That's to come.

Rest and Retirement, Part 2: Jubilee

or: A biblical justification for taking a whole year off

It seems surprising that some of the most progressive labour laws should be found in a document that's over 3000 years old during a time when the vast majority lived on the poverty line and one bad crop meant starvation and death. So look up Leviticus 25. Go on. Get a Bible and look it up. Found it? Isn't it extraordinary?

Okay, for those too lazy to get their Bibles, and those who are reading this whilst on the loo (which is most of you) and to those who, bafflingly, don't have a copy of the book that has the most influence on our culture bar none, let me give you a summary of Leviticus 25: 'Don't just take a Sabbath day. Take a Sabbath year, O Israel! You, your animals and the land could do with a year off. And don't worry – the land will produce enough food for *three* years. I am the LORD. (And I released you from Egpyt and provided for you in the desert. Remember the manna from heaven? And the quails? Seriously. Trust me.) And every seventh Sabbath year, call it a Jubilee and give everything back, return to your place of origin and start all over again.'

If you are reading this book, you are among the wealthi-est people in the world, and in human history. You may find these verses disturbing and scary. This is radical wealth distribution and for most of us the wealth will be flowing outwards and not inwards. But this just shows that we haven't understood the generosity, grace and kindness of God. Thankfully, there's no consensus on how this law should apply to Christians today, so we're all very well protected from God's grace and kindness for now.

But while we work it out, I propose a limited cultural Jubilee for 2013. In that year, all books, CDs and DVDs shall be returned to their original owner. And not only that. *No* new books, CDs, DVDs or Apps shall be produced. You shall not use Garageband, Final Draft, Final Cut or Adobe Photoshop to create new works. TV and recording studios shall remain fallow. You shall not upgrade your smartphone. No one shall write a new book, nor even blog. You shall not order anything from Amazon or iTunes. You may use Spotify, listen to all the music on your iPod, read all those books you already have, and watch those films you taped off ITV2 last Christmas.

Worth a go, surely? In the returning of property, hopefully my DVD of Season 5 of *Seinfeld* that I lent to someone (no idea who) will be returned. Yes, I know I should have written it down. It might also mean the return of at least a dozen umbrellas, gloves and hats that I've left on various modes of transport over the last six years. Have I turned this Jubilee into a general Lost Property session?

But let's face it. We all own books we bought on the spur of the moment but currently have no intention of reading – especially 'improving' books. I have a good number of second-hand books by authors I should have read but haven't. As a result, copies of *War and Peace*, *The Brothers Karamazov* and *A Tale of Two Cities* sit on the shelf staring at me. For those of us who are Christians, a good number of books are purchased just after a spiritual high. With good intentions we resolved to read some proper books, which, in my case, accounts for the John Stott and C. S. Lewis tomes currently unread on my shelf. Plus, in order to understand Islam, I bought a copy of the *Koran* and a decent biography of Mohammed. Untouched. Add to this the books I never had any intention of reading but was given them for Christmas. So add *The Alan Clarke Diaries*, *The Planets* by David Sobel and *The Naked Jape* by Jimmy Carr – which all sound really good, but, y'know … Then there are books like the one by Carl Hiassen that I bought second hand the other day that I was told I'd like. (Update: I have since read it. It was fine.)

It would be wonderful to have a year off working to catch up on my reading, but I only stand a chance of doing that if no new books are published. And it's even more important that film production is also suspended for a year. That way, I stand a fighting chance of clearing my Sky Plus back-catalogue. I currently have *Magnolia*; *It Happened One Night*; *From Here to Eternity*; *Enemy at the Gates*; *Slumdog Millionaire*; *The 40 Year-Old Virgin* to name but a few. And why watch Spielberg's latest offering when I've never even seen *Schindler's List*? This is particularly surprising given that I own a copy. Sadly it's on VHS – as are my unseen copies of *Jaws*, *Psycho* and *The Shining* – and I don't have a video player any more. In fact, there are plenty of classics I haven't seen. A Jubilee would make me ask myself why I'm so keen to watch the latest Will Ferrell comedy when I haven't even seen all of Peter Sellers' classics.

Even better, if I stopped work as a comedy writer for a Sabbath year, I could take the time to see how it's meant to be done by watching Bob Hope, Steven Wright, Jack Benny and Bill Hicks. And who knows? In that year of Jubilee maybe, just maybe, I'll get round to reading the rest of Leviticus.

Haves and Have-Nots, Part 2: Extremes of Wealth

or: How I learnt about money at the Races

One of the things people on the Left like to do is talk about the rich getting richer and the poor getting poorer. They also like blending abstract nouns to create couplets like 'Income Injustice' and 'Status Poverty' that are essentially new terms for age-old problems – like not having as much money as other people and feeling bad about it.

People on the Right also talk like this in an attempt to get people to like them. This is because the alternatives sound wrong when you say them out loud. 'A free society will inevitably allow some individuals to have more money than entire countries,' sounds brutally unjust. Likewise, 'It's not about money but quality of life' is breathtakingly patronising.

And yet both statements are broadly true. A free society does, and should, allow individuals to amass enormous fortunes. And a free society allows those people to hoard it, count it, stash it and pass it onto their children if they wish. It's not morally desirable for them or society but if they want to behave like greedy selfish monsters, that's a shame but their right. But that's the price of freedom and it's not for the State to take it all away. Tax, fine. Inheritance tax, if you must. But simply taking property because it's handy is the sort of thing Robert Mugabe does and it tends not to end well, for the country at least (although Mugabe has done very nicely for himself over the last thirty years).

Moreover, numerous studies demonstrate that the link between money and quality of life is tenuous. And if Hollywood rags-to-riches-to-rags tales are to be believed, taking away everything from a multi-millionaire causes the most giddying happiness of all, causing you to burst into song, hug surprised strangers and smile at the sky with hands aloft shouting inanities: 'Hello, World!', 'I'm alive!' and 'Every day is the first day of the rest of my life!' Then again, Hollywood rags-to-riches-to-rags tales are not to be believed. Although they tap into a truth we all know – that money does not bring happiness.

I mention this because of a lecture I heard at the Greenbelt Festival, a Christian Arts festival which takes place every year at Cheltenham Racecourse. The lecture was by Dr Richard Wilkinson, co-author of the book, *The Spirit Level: Why Equality is Better for Everyone*. The book looks at numerous statistics to show that societies with the greatest disparities in income are, broadly, unhappier because of crime, poorer health and other measures. There were lots of graphs. It was like a Dave Gorman show without the jokes. But it was thorough. And very convincing.

You're expecting a 'but', aren't you? Be honest. You thought I was about to attempt to deny this overwhelming body of statistical evidence. He seemed a little hazier on the reason for this correlation, but there certainly appears to be a strong link between 'Wealth Imbalance' and 'Societal anti-cohesion', to use two more terms I've just made up.

Dr Wilkinson was very keen to prove his point, and mentioned a few times that those on the political right were always keen to deny his findings. Capitalist free-marketeers naturally don't like the idea that the accumulation of wealth without bringing the poor with you is bad for society as a whole. Certainly, it's an unattractive side-effect of unfettered capitalism. Plus free-marketeers like to talk about wealth creation having a 'trickle down' effect, in that rich individuals spend money and so we all get the benefits of that. It sounds reasonable although I'm told that the evidence for it is very scant.

I wouldn't argue for unfettered capitalism anyway because when the markets are fully free, human nature kicks in and, in short, we love a bargain. If we can get something cheaper, we will. This drives down costs and wages, and creates profits for some – and pay cuts for others. But these transactions cannot and should never be done in a moral vacuum. Everything is moral. Dunderheaded bankers who nearly drove the economy off a cliff said 'We didn't do anything wrong.' Legally, they are right. They did not break the law. Just because something isn't a crime, it doesn't make it right.

The only question is how moral are we prepared to be? Taxation won't get to the heart of the problem. It is compulsory so it lets people off the moral hook. We, as a society, need to change the way we think about money, and should be prepared to pay people a decent wage for an honest day's work – and the price of goods should reflect that.

Looking round the lecture hall (well, horses' enclosure), I saw the problem and solution all around me – and sitting in my seat. Christians should be able to see that all things are moral, and that we are all under obligation to care for the poor. But churches and Christian organisations are often the worst at paying people a decent wage for an honest day's work. When we get our own house in order, maybe things will change.

The Theory of Money, Part 3: Labour

or: What you can and cannot put a price on

It's always galling when politicians club together and start clubbing private companies for wasting money. MPs have been calling on G4S to forgo their £57 million fee after their high-profile Olympics blunder in which they failed to recruit enough security staff and had to be bailed out by the Armed Forces. But G4S's main error is that they weren't anywhere near clever enough to get away with wasting such a small amount of money. The politicians, masters of misdirection, know how to waste so much more with much greater subtlety.

So let us remember two numbers. When the games were won for London, the budget was £2.4 billion. Bafflingly, VAT and the security costs were omitted from this. But when the games *were* held, the budget was £11 billion. You have to admire the cheek. In June 2012, the government had the nerve to announce that the games were *under* budget by £476 million, omitting to mention the original budget had been inflated by £9 billion. And then there's the imaginary economic benefits that they always claim, and yet have not one shred of evidence for. But let us generously turn a blind eye to that dishonesty.

I'm not arguing that the games should not have been held. But it's worth remembering that the costs were wildly underestimated. And the costs would have been even greater were it not for the army of volunteers (as well as the army of actual soldiers) who were rightly applauded for their efforts. They were a marked contrast from the posturing magnanimity of the corporate sponsors who only put in £2 billion of the £11 billion budget, although you'd assumed they'd paid for everything given the fawning praise and thanks they received at every turn.

One legacy of the Olympics is, perhaps, the shot in the arm that it has given to the idea of 'volunteering'. And one could be forgiven for thinking that this idea could be folded into some kind of political philosophy. But of course it already has been. It was called the Big Society. It's a perfectly decent idea, albeit ill-defined and half-baked. It sounds something like this: 'Real change is not what government can do on its own – real change is when everyone pulls together, comes together, works together, where we all exercise our responsibilities to ourselves, to our families, to our communities and to others.' These are perfectly reasonable words.

But David Cameron said them. He's an old Etonian who became a Tory Prime Minister so all self-respecting people have to despise this silly nonsensical statement. The very words 'Big Society' are associated with private wealth, public schools, powerful friends and tax avoidance. 'The Big Society' is just a fig leaf for tax cuts so the wealthy can all go out and buy a slightly bigger yacht. So whatever they say, we're against it. At least, this is the childish attitude taken by many of the people I follow on Twitter, many of whom are witty, influential opinion-formers.

When certain news stories crop up, vitriolic flaming jibes are fired at the straw men of the Right along the lines of 'Where's your stupid capitalism now?' and 'The market will never help people like these.' Their assumption is that the Right believe that the unfettered market will solve *all* of society's ills and that they therefore cannot believe in volunteering or the Big Society or even the state. But the Right understand markets – but also the *limits* of market, just as it understands the limits of the state. Or at least it should.

Matters are not helped by statistics presented in a profoundly unhelpful way. The charity Carers UK and the University of Leeds, estimated that 6.4 million people in the UK are providing care for ill, elderly or disabled loved ones. That's one person in ten and no great surprise, surely? They went on to say that this voluntary care would otherwise cost the state 'a staggering £119 billion every year'. Why would you put it in these terms, unless you thought that the state should be caring for every single person in need for every hour of every day? And not even the most die-hard unreconstructed socialist would argue for this dehumanised state of affairs, would they?

Caring for an elderly parent, or someone who is ill or disabled is a serious task. It is something we can choose not to do. But doing it is not ultimately 'saving the state money' or even volunteering. It's called being a parent, or a responsible child, or a brother or sister, friend or neighbour. Ultimately, it's being human – or at least being the people we were created to be. Christians do not have the monopoly on volunteering, but we do believe in a God of Grace who freely gives of himself. And you cannot put a price on that.

Part Three:
The State, Politics
and all things
Governmental

*'Government has become
ungovernable; that is, it cannot
leave off governing. Law has
become lawless; that is, it cannot
see where laws should stop. The
chief feature of our time is the
meekness of the mob and the
madness of the government.'*
G. K. Chesterton, Eugenics and
Other Evils: An Argument Against
the Scientifically Organized State

Journalists and commentators love to talk about 'Postcode Lotteries'. For those unfamiliar with tedious, lazy, UK-hack-speak it's 'The quality of the service you get depends on where you live'. It is most often applied to the NHS and the fact that service is variable in different parts of the country is considered a national catastrophe and an affront to the taxpayer. Sadly, this sentiment is both prevalent and insane.

Let's approach this from both angles. If you're a really good doctor, better than average (I'm sure that includes most doctors, obviously), you have just created a postcode lottery. Someone in a different part of the country will get worse care than the care you provide. There is no way this can be avoided. A postcode lottery is an unavoidable fact.

Equally, if you live in different parts of the country, you will enjoy different benefits. If you're a resident of the Highlands of Scotland you get clear air, stunning views and relatively few public buses. If you live in London, you get buses, tubes, trams and trains, but little in the way of bracken-covered, snow topped mountains. You will get nightlife, an exposure to different cultures and a feeling of being at the centre of things. But you will get dirty air, casual violence and serious parking problems.

But we don't want to live in a postcode lottery, do we? No! Why should the people of Streatham be denied a view of Loch Lomond? Why should I have to go without that excellent doctor who practices in Middlesbrough? Why should I not have Melton Mowbray pork pies made on my doorstep? Isn't this the twenty-first century? Why is society so grossly unfair? Something must be done.

It's daft, and yet we, as British people, will give limitless power and money to Westminster so that they can 'even everything out', passing laws and spending zillions of pounds making everything fair. This cannot be done. Especially not by our politicians of all people.

Attempts at uniformity imply that the state can create a fair society with taxation and legislation. They can't. This is the underlying premise of the following section (and large parts of the previous one). So now we get round to discussing the grubby business of politics. We shall wonder together why we give far too much power to people we don't respect, don't listen to and ultimately can't abide. We also give party politics and conferences a bit of a kicking along with honourable mentions for Tony Benn, William Wilberforce and St George.

The Pomposity of Politicians, Part 1

or: Why I love Tony Benn, even though he's wrong about everything

I'm a fan of Tony Benn. Who isn't? He's a national treasure, along with Lords Cricket Ground, Radio 4 and Boots the Chemist. Coach parties should be organised to Benn's house – for which he would, no doubt, whip up a batch of brownies and tell stories about the time he got to choose the stamp designs as Postmaster General. When he dies, he should be put on permanent display, possibly on the fourth plinth in Trafalgar Square.

I also happen to believe that Tony Benn is wrong about virtually everything. For a start, he believes in planned economies and the nationalisation of, well, most things: car production; potatoes; Newton's Laws of Physics. He'd merrily centralise the distribution of butter, paperclips and sprouts. Ultimately, he believes in government. And doesn't believe in the market. The point is, he believes in some things. And not other things.

Do you remember when politicians had beliefs? You know, strong convictions that they actually talked about? In front of other people? In public? This is why I am a fan of Tony Benn. He's stuck to his guns, and when popular opinion moved away from his views, he kept the same views because he thought they were right. And he didn't, and still doesn't, care what other people think.

Granted, it can be a worry when heavily-armed people don't care what other people think (see George W. Bush, Robert Mugabe, Saruman and his Orcs, etc.). But we don't need to worry about Tony Benn on this front. Moreover, it is not intrinsically virtuous to stand up and say things people think are stupid or dangerous like Nick Griffin does all the time, like Noel Edmonds does in his anti-PC Sky show *Noel's HQ*, which is *That's Life*-meets-*Nuremburg*.

But politics is, or should be, about standing up and making a case for a political ideology. It should be a quest to persuade the people that your way of thinking is a better way than theirs. And that you should be elected to enact those policies, rather than someone else's. And if you can't persuade them, sit down. It's not your turn. So, what should happen is something along these lines:

Would-be MP: I believe in devolving powers to an ultra-local level, which would give us greater community and accountability! Yes, it would mean regional variation, but isn't that the case across the world in general? Isn't a locally-run world a better one? Vote for me!

Listener: No! I want a centrally-planned economy with no regional variation. Pipe down. I'm voting for the other guy.

Would-be MP: Oh, well that's what I believe. Are you sure I can't persuade you to devolve power to local communities?

Listener: Not really. We are quite fixed on having a centrally-planned economy. No offence.

Would-be MP: None taken. I'll go.

Listener: Yup. Okay then. Ask Mrs Wilson for a cup of tea. I'm sure there's some left in the pot.

Would-be MP: Decent of you. Well, bye, then.

But when you abandon the concept of conviction, what actually happens, regardless of party, is this:

Would-be MP: I want you to vote for me, because I listen to your views!

Listener: Well, we want a centrally-planned economy.

Would-be MP: Hey! Me too! Spooky. Vote for me.

Listener: Oh. What if I'd said I believe that bull-fights should be held in Trafalgar Square and that the NHS should be scrapped?

Would-be MP: I'd have agreed with that too. The important thing is that I'm the guy that listens and does what you say.

Listener: Well, hang on. You're not really adding anything to this.

Would-be MP: Oh, come come. I'm great. I have a family. I'm not corrupt and I've been successful in business, but not so much that you want to hate me. So you should vote for me. Seriously. Because Britain will be better as long as I'm in charge.

Listener: So what will you do when you get into power?

Would-be MP: All that stuff you said. And other stuff. Not sure. I'll probably ask you again. Is that okay?

Listener: Sounds perfect. Hooray for democracy.

It's horrible. We're stuck in a vicious feedback-loop of politicians trying to sell prejudice and pragmatism back to their own people, because everyone's afraid of saying what they actually think. The contest between the parties is not who has the best policies, but who has the most accurately calibrated focus groups.

When William Wilberforce stood up in the House of Commons to argue for the abolition of slavery, most of Parliament thought he was mad. Or dreaming. But he believed in his cause. He sought to persuade others. Slowly, gradually, he did so. And eventually succeeded. What Britain needs in these troubled times is not mealy-mouthed pseudo-socialist pragmatism. It needs – and always will need – men and women with policy, principle and genuine courage.

The Problem of Patriotism

or: Why flying a St George's flag shouldn't make you feel like a racist (even though it does)

St Patrick's Day is a cheerful, boozy affair, full of Guinness and good will. St David's Day is a jolly day too, with its curious blend of daffodils, leeks and red dragons. St Andrew seems to have been usurped by Rabbie Burns *and* Hogmanay. Fair enough. But the Scots have their day. Two, in fact.

But what about the English? How should they celebrate their national day? Obvious traditions would be gathering around Nelson's Column – or makeshift versions of the same in town squares up and down the land – singing 'Jerusalem' by Blake and then 'Vindaloo' by Fat Les before someone reads out Henry V's Agincourt speech, a claim is made on behalf of the Crown for the French throne and the Tricolour is solemnly set on fire. (Come on, would it kill the French to at least hand back Calais?) Then it's all down to the local pub to watch a big-screen football match in which England lose to Germany on penalties.

Instead the English are far more comfortable playing it down, and worrying about whether flying a St George flag will cause offence. The flag makes some uncomfortable as it has those 'Eng-er-land' nationalistic overtones. But then, isn't that what you'd want on your national day? Apparently not. The problem is that St George's flag has other associations: that of a crusading knight.

All of this is beautifully riddled with irony upon irony which is convenient given that quietly appreciating irony is a popular English pastime. One irony, though, is that irony is now used to denote something that technically isn't irony. But we digress. There is irony all over the St George's Flag/Englishness debate.

Irony One is that England has produced a number of fine Christian men who would make more suitable Patron saints than St George – who is not even English. Should George have to re-apply for his own job, he would have to see off Aquinas and Anselm, who would surely be on the shortlist (with Edward the Confessor and Thomas a Becket on the long list).

Irony Two is that England has been a Protestant country for nearly five hundred years – so we don't really *do* canonisation and saints. In the Protestant denomination, all Christians are considered saints, since this is how the New Testament most commonly uses the term. So all English Christians could lay claim to being an English saint. This would fit well with the times. Just as *Time* Magazine Person of the Year in 2006 was 'You', what better way for a self-obsessed, narcissistic population to celebrate itself than by making 'Everyone' a patron saint of England 2.0? Wow, just typing that makes me feel slightly unwell.

Irony Three is that St George famously slew a dragon. Dragons, it hardly needs saying, no longer exist. And this seems unlikely to be St George's fault. There is no evidence that he hunted them to extinction, not least because dragons have never existed. Irony Three Subsection One is that the dragon is the symbol of the Welsh, so right away the English have a saint who is crassly offensive to neighbouring inhabitants of their own island.

Irony Four is that St George's flag has associations with crusaders. Crusades were, of course, launched *against* the Turks and St George was probably Turkish. How fitting that England has a patron saint who is primarily in conflict with himself.

So can we fly the flag of St George for a day without being considered a White Van Man – or one of those people who say things like 'It's not racist for wanting preferential treatment for the British' when that is, in fact, a really good definition of racism? What is a Christian response to this dilemma, given that Christians are citizens of heaven – where there will be people of every nation, tribe and tongue?

What's the real issue here? It's the same issue that's behind why at every sporting contest the Scots will support *anyone* against the English. The English have traditionally been the dominant power within Britain, asserting themselves over the Welsh, the Scots and particularly the Irish, sometimes with shameful brutality. What's more, the English, as the dominant power within Britain, have flexed their muscles all over the world. Less than a hundred years ago, the British Empire covered a quarter of the world's land and population; 458 million were under the Union Jack – which, at the centre, has St George's Cross.

How we respond to this dilemma rather depends on your attitude to power. And St George is a brilliant example of how Christians should behave in positions of power. He was a Roman soldier, probably a tribune, and as such must have felt unstoppable. But he was a Christian. And when an edict came that all Christians in the army should offer a sacrifice to pagan Gods, he didn't hold onto that power. He gave it up and was executed. Does that sound like anyone else? (Hint: His name begins with 'J'.) The flag of St George may be associated with intolerant military strength but there is also a wonderful blood-red, cross-shaped streak of Christian humility.

Politics and Privacy, Part 1

or: How a government can send you so many forms to fill in (and yet still claim to not know where you live)

There are numerous contradictions in life in a modern state, but we have learned to live with them. Annually, we fill in dozens of forms for state bodies like the NHS, the DVLA and the Council; we are sent incomprehensible documents from the Child Tax Credit office, council tax bills and angry letters from the TV Licence people; and yet the government insist they have no idea of who we are or where we live. And so every ten years, we have to fill another form called a census.

The results of this census, we're told, are used for planning and the provision of services. We are filmed out and about in the street by hundreds of thousands of CCTV cameras, photographed in our cars by speed cameras and use our credit cards to buy train tickets – and yet the government has no idea how many of us need to get to work and how we'll get there.

Such information is already available given the dozens of government bureaucracies and databases. One would imagine it would be easy to save us all the bother of another form to fill with some kind of national database with all these details already collated and processed. But on reflection that could easily lead to exactly the madness that George Orwell would write about.

I'm not arguing that the census is another example of a police state that already knows far too much about us. Our state doesn't resemble a Stasi officer with a million meticulously-kept deadly accurate files on every single one of us. Our state is more like a slightly baffled old man with a selectively fabulous memory – with panic attacks and the unshakeable conviction that he is right. In many ways, the latter is a worse combination – since it combines amnesia and paranoia with coercive violence.

Thankfully, the Coalition government has already scrapped the idea of a national database and identity cards. One would like to think it was due to political conviction and a belief in civil liberty. But it was probably cost. Like all hopelessly conceived, poorly executed government IT projects, things were escalating out of control. And we all know the punchline. Sooner or later, an anonymous civil servant would put the entire database onto a memory stick and then leave it on the 17.05 from Kings Cross.

It's ironic the civil servants in these cases are always anonymous. I don't expect people to be tarred and feathered, but accountability is critical, and absent. Prising information out of any government body is virtually impossible. In *The Silent State*, journalist Heather Brook documents how politicians in Seattle publish all their expenses claims online in the most drearily accurate and un-newsworthy way.

In Britain, Brook found that civil servants demand secrecy while they spend more taxpayers' money on press officers to keep journalists away from discovering any wasteful embarrassment. Meanwhile, MPs demand privacy right up to the point that they wish to take credit for courageously spending taxpayers' money on another short-term initiative. We have to fill in a form to find out any details about any of the above through the Freedom of Information Act. And in the meantime, we have to fill in a form giving them all our information again. Failure to do so truthfully is, in fact, an offence. The census is just another classic example of the state doing what it does best – making us pay full attention while it wastes our time and money.

It's also a waste because the information collected is barely of any use. The religious question on the form is a good example, having been written by a civil servant who has clearly never met a religious person. There is one box for Christianity. One box. All Christians are, according to the Anglican Protestant state, the same. It may be frustrating and embarrassing that Christians have spent hundreds of years arguing about Protestantism and Catholicism, but one must admit that if Christians *themselves* can't agree on what a Christian is, what chance does the state have? And what about Mormons? Christian Scientists? Jehovah's Witnesses? Will they be included in the final tally? Who decides? We have no way of knowing.

But by far the biggest group are those people who consider themselves culturally Christian, but not 'practising'? The British Humanist Association were very keen such people say they have 'no religion', mainly to stop Christian groups from crowing that 'most people in this country say they are Christian' and demanding rights accordingly.

One has to wonder how successful the humanist campaign will be. Lots of people say that they're not religious, but to take a pen and tick a box that states you 'have no religion' is further than some may be prepared to go because they have a sneaking suspicion that, despite those hundreds of years of bickering over Catholicism and Protestantism, ultimately there still may be something in it.

The Pointlessness of the Party Conference, Part 1

or: Why we should all listen to Radio 3 in September

Recently, I have been having breakfast to the sound of BBC Radio 3. There are a number of reasons for this. The first is that I like classical music. The Radio 3 breakfast show is not for die-hard purists though, playing single movements and shorter pieces, making at least some concession to the time of day. (No one's got the best part of an hour to listen to Mahler's Fifth while eating cornflakes. That many corn-flakes is very unhealthy.)

The second reason is that I have small children, and being a middle class parent, I am keen to make my four-year old and two-year old appreciate The Arts whilst they have no choice in the matter.

But the third reason is that the show is mostly music, and very little talking. In particular, there is very little news. Radio 3 would always rather talk about a composer who died in 1871, than a politician who's desperately trying to get us to eat healthily or vote for them. On Radio 3, one can avoid the tedious, playground taunting that passes for inter-views on Radio 4. One can avoid the incessant reading out of knee-jerk texts and emails from uninformed listeners on Five Live. It's lovely.

Radio 3 really comes into its own in September, when party conferences are in full swing. The Media loves to give these events their full attention and hours of coverage and analysis, but they are completely self-defeating.

A party conference can only have two real purposes. The first is a feel-good knees-up with back-slapping speeches where politicians queue up to offer their praise to each other. The party faithful get to feel like they're part of things and everyone goes home happy, inspired and unchallenged. A bit like a Sunday church service when it's not quite doing its job. (It's fine to be inspired, but we all know there's more to it than that.)

The second more useful purpose of a party conference is an introspective search for the party's soul. Difficult questions should be asked. Deep philosophical issues should be raised, and then examined, discussed and debated well into the night with a single malt (with someone sober taking notes in case the single malt wins the argument on the night).

The problem, as we have said, is that party conferences are open to the media, and frequently broadcast to the nation – or at least the parts of the nation whose TVs are stuck on BBC2 and can't seem to get their Freeview/Sky box to change channel. Because the politicians feel under the glare of the nation's gaze, they act on their mistaken view that the nation likes to see parties united. In the past, for example, Tories have thought people won't vote for them if they appear divided on the issue of Europe. In fact, those who don't vote Tory do so for a variety of gut-felt, prejudicial or intellectual reasons, good and bad. Division over Europe is not really one of them.

Divisions within religions usually look bad, especially when they end in obscene and hateful language or bloodshed. But everyone expects politicians to at least resort to the former, so why the big deal over presenting a united front over everything?

The result is a self-defeating party conference in which every speech given is designed to have four qualities; vague acceptability to the people in the room; a blandness that it appears is part of mainstream policy and therefore makes the party look united; a lack of gaffes to avoid the attention of the journalists who will report verbal slips with pathetic childish glee; and an appeal to the people who aren't there and were never going to vote for them anyway. In short, it's like trying to conduct a Presbyterian church service, in a synagogue, live on Al Jazeera. It is, at best, a waste of time.

Party conferences should be private affairs, with doors closed and the press excluded. Politicians, SPADs and wonks should lock themselves in a big room and work out what they're about and why – while the rest of us listen to Mahler's Fifth eating cornflakes, which can't be any harder work than watching *The Daily Politics* during conference season.

Politics and Privacy, Part 2

or: Why supermarkets know much more about me than the State (and why this isn't altogether a bad thing)

'The past is a foreign country,' wrote L. P. Hartley. 'They do things differently there.' They certainly do. Three hundred and fifty years ago, the English were embroiled in civil war. Men killed each other sparked by public, vocal and passionate arguments about the nature of government. Imagine that. The English discussing the nature of government publicly, vocally and passionately. It doesn't happen anymore. In about 1650, we discovered that this was a debate not worth having too often. Consequently, our current government doesn't talk about it. It's a shame, as important questions need to be answered. Here's one. Who are you? And who says so? And who says who says so? And who decided that? Okay, that's four questions but they stem from the first one. They are about personal identity.

As things stand, you are a series of numbers: a passport number; a driving licence number; a home number; a mobile number; an IP address number; a tax number; a national insurance number; a credit card number; an expiry date; and, if your bank still exists when you're reading this chapter, an account number, a sort code and a PIN.

Despite this dazzling array of identifiers (and the trusty gas bill), some politicians still think it's well worth spending billions of pounds on another series of numbers that will officially dignify us with existence. This issue comes round every five years or so, usually during a time of national paranoia after a terrorist event. New Labour spent a lot of money on it.

Home Secretary Jacqui Smith got as far as unveiling the design for the card which bore the title 'residence permit.' It was a bland, pink and blue thing with some numbers, your picture and a small outline of a bull. Was the bull a visual representation of our government charging at full speed in the wrong direction in a way that is likely to be very damaging, harmful and expensive? Or was the bull just a euphemism?

She was just one of a number of ministers who trotted out numerous arguments in favour of the ID-card scheme. It will help prevent terrorism, they say. Which it won't, since they also said the scheme would be voluntary. There is no spectre of the Big Brother state, they claim. Or selling the information to big businesses. There'd be no point. Tesco already know far more about me than the government ever would. In terms of information, Tesco are infinitely more qualified than the government to know where to build hospitals, schools, dental practices and roads.

But these are mostly pragmatic concerns, not philosophical ones. The question proponents of identity cards need to answer is much more fundamental. 'Why should the State be the ones to confer identity?' Have you ever heard any politician begin to try and answer that question?

When my wife and I named our daughter, we were obliged to tell the state within six weeks. Strangely enough, we drew little enjoyment from her name being tapped into a computer in Chelsea Town Hall. We were more thrilled when she was baptised into the church in her name a few months later. God seems to let parents get on with naming their children without form-filling, paperwork or databases (unless you're about to conceive a messiah in which case an angel will set you right). Sadly our State, which believes it can raise and educate our children, is rapidly assuming His role whilst perpetually claiming to be secular. They're lying.

The Pomposity of Politicians, Part 2

or: Why it's a shame that there's no longer any shame

We do not live in a shame culture. Which is a shame. Honour seems to be a luxury in our current age. There is a saying that we get the politicians we deserve. If that were so, we would be able to see this shamelessness in our elected representatives. And we do. Everywhere.

What does it take to get a government minister to resign? In the 1980s, not very much. Politicians used to resign on principle quite regularly. A whiff of a scandal, a rogue civil servant, financial impropriety or even differences of policy would trigger the minister handing in their notice. The minister would be pictured on the Six O'Clock News walking out of 10 Downing Street smiling at the cameras and vowing to spend more time with his family while sitting on the back benches.

Let us take a moment to recall some of the 1980's resignations. Heseltine walked out over a helicopter manufacturer, Westland. Nicholas Ridley went over some unfortunate comments about Germany and the EU in *The Spectator*. Nigel Lawson quit over differences of opinion about monetarism. Sir Geoffrey Howe resigned because he just couldn't bear the Prime Minister any more. By today's standards, these are footling issues.

In the 1990s, things were far more tawdry, with plenty of scandals about extra-marital affairs, illegitimate children and dodgy dealings. Take a trip down memory lane by googling Tim Yeo, Neil Hamilton and Jonathan Aitken. Then there was Alan Clark who scandalised everyone with his candour and shameless talk. But, surprisingly, it was mostly talk.

Perhaps a new kind of rot set in with David Mellor who clung on to his ministerial post, despite being caught with his trousers down while his party was espousing back-to-basics family values. The result of this gross hypocrisy was that he became a laughing stock for many years to come and brought shame upon his party, the government and the nation. He should have resigned.

Sadly, New Labour took after Mellor's example and turned clinging on to a ministerial job into an art form, as have the current administration. The following should trigger your memory: Keith Vaz; Jo Moore; Stephen Byers; Martin Sixsmith; Ecclestone and F1; the Hinduja brothers; Mandelson (twice); Robinson; Blunkett; Prescott; McBride; Jacqui Smith; and Cash for Honours. Oh, and that war. And then, Dr Liam Fox and his buddy, and Jeremy Hunt and Murdoch.

There was never any question of these ministers resigning over policy. All politicians pride themselves on ideological flexibility (see The Pomposity of Politicians Part 1). Nor is there any prospect of quitting over stories of massive incompetence since this pouring of billions down the drain (mostly into IT projects) can blamed on a series of predecessors and curiously nameless bureaucrats. The only crime in politics is being caught doing something indefensible with government funds (or on a government desk), and even then the penalties can sometimes be avoided.

In fact, the shameful impropriety can be turned into a post-political D-List celebrity career. The Hamiltons can milk their brown envelope schtick on the panto circuit. Lord Prescott can make money out of commercials making jokes about his misuse of two unnecessarily expensive cars and punching a member of the public in the face.

The sad situation is that honour and shame have flown away. Stories about misuse of power, inappropriate loans, expenses scandals and unprofessional behaviour have to run in the press for weeks at fever pitch before the minister in question eventually caves in, issues a half-apology with a bunch of excuses before stepping down and waiting for his turn to come round again.

I mention this because the cockles of my heart were warmed during the St Paul's protest debacle. Within days of a rumpus, Canon Giles Fraser, Chancellor of the Cathedral resigned on principle, with a passionate official statement that contained the words 'complete nonsense'. Sensational. A few days later, the Dean fell on his sword – and the Bishop said the Dean had 'acted honourably'. I hope you saw that, Westminster. Whatever else comes of this strange spectacle, the church has been showing the way on how to resign: quickly, with honour and *con brio*. Amen to that.

The Prejudice of the Political Parties

or: How to write off your opponents in one easy step

About a decade ago, bookshops began selling large numbers of books that had black or red covers, with red, black or white writing on the front. Klein's *No Logo*, Monbiot's *Captive State* and Bakan's *The Corporation*. I read a few of them. I even took a discounted subscription for *New Statesman* (which is also red, white and black).

I began to flag whilst reading Schlosser's *Fast Food Nation*. Soon I realised the low whining sound in my ears was not tinnitus but a mental condition picked up from prolonged exposure to books by Klein, Monbiot and company. (Oops. Not 'company'. Companies are bad. They can lead to oppression. Compatriots? Oops. No. Patriotism is bad too. Can lead to racism. Comrades?) Ultimately, I just didn't agree with their view of the role of the state. And this affects everything. They assume all decent people want an interventionist state. They believe the government should provide things and plan economies. They are on the Left. I am not.

Now, whenever I see a book with a black cover, a white blob and some red writing, I tend not to bother with it. Daniel Finkelstein, of *The Times*, has his own system. The warning sign is a positive quote from Noam Chomsky on the cover. A recommendation from Chomsky renders the book unworthy of his precious time.

The Finkelstein system has the danger of doing to the Left what the Left enjoys doing to the Right. Labelling them. Labels are a powerful and deceitful way of removing someone from a debate, or writing them off. Sir Humphrey Appleby explains this to Bernard in *Yes, Prime Minister*. A fervent Christian is in line to be the next Governor of the Bank of England, so Sir Humphrey encourages labelling him, calling him 'a lay preacher' and 'a zealot' knowing that such terms are essentially smears in the political arena.

The Left has been wonderfully successful in its labelling. Their smearing is second to none. In fact, it is now socially impossible to stand on the Right without shame or fear. Right Wing = reactionary = conservative = capitalist = fascist = racist. If you are one of those things, you're most likely to be all of them. It's a triumph of spin and language.

'Fascist' is a wonderful, visceral word that trips off the tongue beautifully. The 'F' makes it sounds like a swearing. Fascist. The next step is to call them a Nazi, joke about the trains running on time and then draw swastikas on their literature. They hate that. Because it works. It's so effective it is now widely believed that the Right must be Wrong simply because they are Fascists. Which they are not. Margaret Thatcher was accused of being a Fascist 25 years ago when she took on the miners. Which she was not.

I personally oppose an interventionist state. My understanding of the Bible is that the State has *only* a magisterial role to which all citizens, Christians and all, must submit. Beyond that the state has zero legitimate function. That puts me on the political Right. Why, then, must the deeply offensive assumption be that I am fascist. And therefore a racist? I am neither. I quite like England. I find jokes about the French funny. That's about as far as it goes.

I remember learning about Nazis at school – and hearing that the word is short for 'National Socialists'. Socialists. How can the Nazis be socialists if they're on the Far Right? Maybe the label is the problem. There is an excellent book out there called *Liberal Fascism* by Jonah Goldberg who points out the glaringly obvious that is always ignored. Nazis were, of course, fascists. They were *also* racists. Mussolini, the darling of the *Left* in America for many years (until about September 1939) was a proper fascist – he practically invented it – but even he couldn't understand Hitler's extreme racism. Mussolini believed in revolution and the imposition of the state through violence. But why pick on people because of their race? Shalom Auslander says 'Racism makes no sense. There are so many reasons to dislike people … you're going to go with color?'

Ultimately, Fascists, like Communists, consider the State to be our only hope of delivering utopia or heaven today, tomorrow or soon-ish. So everything has to be subservient to the State, especially the church and the family. They advocate spending huge sums of money on vast public works. And they extend the powers of the police, incarcerate suspects without trial and in order to enforce State-based liberty, make certain opinions expressed on social media illegal – or at least worthy of arrest. All sounds familiar.

The Pomposity of Politicians, Part 3

or: Why it's important that the Prime Minister runs the country from a pokey, impractical, terraced house

There are plenty of things that turn me off a country: public spectacles of animal cruelty; a widespread acceptance of sexual harassment; a tradition of men sitting by the door gazing around while the women to do all the work. The one that most worries me, however, is ubiquitous posters of *El Presidente*.

One could argue that Britain is a land of animal cruelty, wolf-whistling, and lazy feckless men. But we certainly don't go in for the kind of brazen self-serving political self-promotion that other nations so readily tolerate. Granted, the Queen's head is on all the stamps and coins, but she is only officially Head of State and doesn't say much otherwise. And she devolves virtually all power to the Prime Minister who acts as the nation's premier.

Since the sheen and lustre came off Tony Blair, the personal rating of our Prime Minister has been pretty low. Let's be honest; those early Blair years were very awkward. Blair was truly popular. And we kept cheering for five years. The vitriol resumed when we realised we had missed out on five years of ridicule and disrespect. We thought Blair was going to actually *do* something with his immense popularity. He could have used his enormous majority to make some unpopular, necessary decisions for the country (like address the pensions time bomb, the unsustainable NHS model, the state-subsidy of family breakdown and suchlike). But he didn't. And when we realised this, we got to be scornful, angry and generally happier. Blair eventually gave way to a widely disliked Brown who presided over a catastrophic economic collapse. He handed over to an old Etonian whose personal rating has never really gone higher than 'reluctantly tolerated'.

The job of being Prime Minister is not one that lends itself to pomp and grandeur. From day one, any new PM is struggling to maintain any kind of dignity because they have to live at 10 Downing Street. On reflection, it seems like utter madness that Britain's most senior politician should run one of the largest economies in the world from a terraced house in Pall Mall. Many heads of state across the world would insist on a palace as a matter of course. Some of the more deranged presidents spend huge sums of public money erecting large golden statues of themselves that will even rotate in order to be beautifully lit by the sun. But if you want to run Britain, you have to live above the shop. On a pokey, dimly-lit street off Whitehall. At Number 10 – not even number 1. (And who is Downing?) The reality is the Prime Minister would have a more comfortable house, and a better salary, as a partner in a small city law firm.

But this is undoubtedly a good thing. It deters people from seeking office for poor motives. The disastrous accommodation and the terrible salary at least flush out those in it for the house or the money. Getting rid of those who want to be Prime Minister because they get a kick out of being in charge is harder. The constant criticism, scrutiny and childish journalists trying to catch them out is a start. But perhaps the Queen could help out here. When she asks David Cameron to form a government in a few years' time, if he says, 'Oh, goodie', or 'You got that right, your maj', or punches the air, Prince Philip will get out the twelve-bore and rid the nation of another grandstander.

Why are the British happy with this extraordinary model of leadership? Can anyone imagine Mugabe or Berlusconi settling for it? They must look in amazement at the British propensity to cry foul in the national press if the Home Secretary so much as secures a parking space for his personal trainer. In some countries, that is simply a privilege of being in office – pulling strings, granting favours and getting cushy jobs for relatives. Moreover, the much monitored American President at least gets to live in the White House and then receive funding for a library. (George W. Bush's is presumably mainly comprised of picture books and *Where's Wally?*)

But we prefer the British way – which is actually a Biblical way. It's how leadership is meant to be, modelled by Christ. Service through humility. Prime Ministerial leadership is not about waving from a car and taking applause. In fact, the Prime Minster has someone to do that for him. She's called The Queen. But it doesn't matter if all the applause goes to her head because she doesn't have any real power. All our current Prime Minister can do is 'get on with the job', which is what Prime Ministers constantly assure us they're doing – from the flat above the office off Pall Mall. Good luck to them.

The Pointlessness of the Party Conference, Part 2

or: How Jesus hates cry-babies

The ugliest thing of 2010 took place during the Conservative Party conference. For some, that'll be no big surprise, although it is not the Tory ministers at fault here. The revolting moment took place after it was suggested, entirely reasonably, that top-rate taxpayers shouldn't receive child benefit.

We must leave aside the colossal administration this will entail, the extra baffling forms that will need to be filled in and the resultant fact that this measure will probably save the nation virtually nothing. It is a sad irony that making sure the wrong people don't get the money costs more money than just letting the wrong people have the money.

The savings are not the point here. The ugliness was in the whingeing and whining and moaning from Middle England. (Not to be confused with Middle Earth, which sounds much nicer, orcs, goblins and wraiths included. Middle Earth doesn't have Melanie Phillips.)

And yet when the plan was floated to withdraw child-benefit from top-rate taxpaying households, the howls could be heard from Hastings to Harrogate. 'We pay taxes too. Shouldn't we get something back?' said the rich. (My answer: I'm not sure you've understood what taxation is.) 'This is penalising those who work hard.' (My answer: The richer should pay more tax. Be grateful you're richer and have a nice job.) But here is most toxic objection: 'What about the couple next door who both earn just below the top-rate threshold? Their combined income will be much higher than my spouses's top-rate income. And yet they'll get child benefit when they clearly don't need it. They already holiday in Tuscany and shop at Waitrose. (At least, their au pair shops at Waitrose for them.) Why should the government pay for Petit Filous for Octavian and Persephone? While my own children, Oliver and Poppy, have to make do with Ski yoghurts from Sainsbury's?'

That, sadly, is the main substance of the objection. Middle England is a nation of envious cry-babies. Sadder still, is that the Tories – and the press – didn't simply laugh at this childish squawking.

So what would be a Christian response to this proposal and subsequent protests? Recently, I've been reading a number of the parables and one theme that comes across is a surprising one: that Jesus hates cry-babies. Jesus doesn't hate those in genuine pain or distress, obviously. But look at his response to the man in Luke 12 who says 'Teacher, tell my brother to divide the inheritance with me.' He does not say 'There, there,'; nor even 'Now you two play nicely.' He tells the man a parable about a rich man who becomes even richer thanks to the good fortune of a good crop. He decides to live the good life. And dies. Jesus gives this man no sympathy, but warns him about being controlled by money and consumed by 'fairness'. This is hardly an isolated parable. There are others in which people who work all day and others who work for only an hour are paid the same wage. The moral of that story is 'Get over it'.

It's a stark contrast to the painstakingly researched, and carefully argued bestseller *The Spirit Level* in which it is proposed that rich people make the rest of us feel bad. And that that's bad and wrong. It's just a nuanced, academic version of the Middle Englanders whining about child benefit cuts.

The national debate has moved on, and so The Right lambast The Undeserving Poor who received benefits with no intention of working. And the left remain obsessed with

The Undeserving Rich, who receive large bonuses regard-less of how hard they work and how they avoid tax.

And yet Jesus refuses to be drawn in to petty arguments about who deserves what, since we don't get what we deserve in this life, for good and ill. From his parables, Jesus' response to the obsessions of the Left and the Right is not to find ways of 'progressive' forced wealth redistribution so that we all have the same and no one feels bad. His solution is the surprising non-political message: 'Get over it'.

Public and Private Healthcare Policy

or: Why this chapter will ensure I can never become Prime Minister

The NHS is like a crap friend. When the chips are really down, they come through for you, but most of the time you feel like slapping them.

Questioning the whole raison d'être of the National Health Service is political suicide, so this chapter marks the end of any ambitions I have in that direction. I would happily celebrate sixty years of the NHS by scrapping it, rendering me unelectable. But before you throw this book across the room, or flush it down the toilet that you might conceivably be sitting on, let me explain my reasoning.

First, let us admit that the NHS is not a health *service* but a health *system*. It's not remotely patient-centred. For our first child, my wife saw over a dozen different midwives in the course of pregnancy, labour and post-natal care. When our new-born baby was readmitted to hospital (a different one, for some reason), we simply couldn't find the baby unit, despite the plethora of signs and maps. And when I thought my daughter's life was in grave danger, traffic wardens were swarming all over the car park like vultures waiting for an animal to die.

For most people, bad experiences like this are quickly erased by the elation of leaving the hospital better, cured, operated on, or with a prescription for restorative drugs. But my experiences have led me to think that the NHS favours the pushy, not the poor, with its byzantine systems, and complex and confusing letters. Unless you can make multiple appointments, telephone numerous departments and endlessly repeat symptoms and stories you may not get the right treatment. In a bid to care for all, the poorly educated and most vulnerable are served worst.

Of course, many people enjoy good service from the NHS. This is because it employs thousands of public-spirited, kind, well-trained and professional doctors, nurses, surgeons, midwives and the like. But since the NHS completely dominates healthcare provision in Britain, there is hardly anywhere else for these good folk to work, even if they wanted to.

Secondly, let us attempt to have an imagination. It's easy if you try. It's surprising how people refuse to consider the alternatives, despite the fact that plenty of developed countries don't have £90-billion health behemoths. But most of us, who are now permanently, intravenously hooked up to state healthcare, only see private healthcare as the alternative and we're sure that this cannot be the answer.

Private healthcare could, in fact, be a large part of the answer. Bear in mind that the NHS costs every man, woman and child £1500 a year. And that a large number of patients just need a reassuring minute or two with a GP, some bed-rest and maybe some antibiotics. This is not an expensive procedure. Most people could afford to pay for even minor operations if they did not have to pay 57 varieties of taxation. Our tax system also serves the poor the worst. Someone working 40 hours a week on minimum wage could afford to pay for GP visits and medicine if the Chancellor of the Exchequer didn't insist on taking £1790 a year in income tax and National Insurance.

Private healthcare also responds better to patients. As a result, where would you rather have a heart bypass? A government hospital. Or a clinic run by John Lewis (with the catering by Waitrose). And hospitals free from government dogma may give you the medicine that will make you better. At the moment, the nice people at NICE decide whether you can have the drugs that decide whether you live or die. You don't get to choose. And you can't pay the difference. No, no. That would be wrong. And your untimely, early death will make that point extremely poignantly.

But private hospitals are run for profit. It's okay for hospitals to profit from sickness, just as supermarkets profit from hunger (see below, *The National Food Service*). But you might be diagnosed with something really serious, and you might not have the right insurance or deep enough pockets to pay. That's why private hospitals are not the whole answer. We need free, or subsidised hospitals too. But who will provide them?

Let's think. Which group in society have a specific mandate for caring for the sick and the poor? Why are nurses called 'sisters'? Why are old hospitals called St Somebody's? Christians used to take care for the sick extremely seriously. Then they discovered they could get the state to do their dirty work. It was around then that people stop taking Christians seriously. The NHS is not only bad for Britain, it's catastrophic for Christendom.

The National Food Service

Imagine a country called The United Isles of Britain. In it, people have very fixed views about what the government should and should not provide. In the UIB, it's food. Everyone agrees that it's the government's job to ensure that no one goes hungry. After all, what could be more important than food? It's a basic requirement for life! Far too important to be left to the market or private food schemes. The UIB thinks its National Food Service is the envy of the world. Food is given out for free to everyone. No one gets special treatment. Everyone gets the same from their local NFS store.

The NFS isn't perfect, of course. It's underfunded – what isn't? Although there has been a recent splurge to ensure that everyone gets better food, and don't have to queue for quite so long. But people put up with the queues. After all, who can tell what people will want to eat? Or which crops grow at which time of the year? Some NFS 'shops' are better than others. Every year league tables are published and shops have various targets to meet. In some parts of the country you can get as many free radishes as you like, which annoys some people who can't get any where they are. In the Scottish part of the UIB, the Associate Food and Nutritional Board have approved the serving of doughnuts, whereas the English Committee for the Approval of Relevant Foodstuffs and Comestibles flatly refuse to give anyone doughnuts – even if money is offered. It's the principle and the government are working to iron out this postcode lottery. After all, everyone in Britain should be entitled to cabbages without waiting for more than six to ten working days.

Of course you can get cabbages on demand in a private shop if you really want one. They cost £61, but they come nicely wrapped and you can eat them in a room by yourself. There aren't that many private shops – after all, who can compete with shops that give out food for free? (Even though you have to wait for a couple of months if you want a parsnip or some Cheerios …) The UIB Food Acquisitions Importation Committee bought 32,000 boxes of Cheerios from the Americans in 2007. They only lasted 2 days (except for the 12,000 that remained in storage in Bristol docks because they did not have the correct documentation).

Some find it easier to go abroad for their food. People call it 'Food tourism'. Thousands of people go to Poland, India or Singapore for their food, sometimes having several complex meals (3 courses!) but it seems a bit of a waste of money when there's perfectly good food available in Britain. Yes, you sometimes find out the potatoes you've been waiting for are rotten, or a sous-chef has left a glove in your fruit salad but mistakes happen.

The only drawback of the NFS is the colossal expense. It costs over £90 billion a year, but there are so many people for the government to pay. Farmers and gardeners, chefs and sous-chefs, shop stackers, cashiers, managers and even some landscape gardeners, although most of them operate privately. Everyone agrees that it could be managed better, and the whole system is constantly being reformed, but their IT bill alone runs into hundreds of millions. There's a new database that records everything you eat, ensuring that you and your kids are getting their allowance, and food groups. If you don't eat properly, they have the state's permission to break your door down and feed you, or take away your children if you're giving them wrong food groups since this is basically child abuse.

The NFS has its critics obviously. Some say that the government has no business dabbling in food production and distribution, but hardly anyone agrees with them, certainly not in public. It's a very sensitive subject. After all, free food for everyone is a wonderful and noble thing. As the Minister for Food in the UIB recently said:

'You can't put a price on that, can you? Food is a basic human necessity and a right. And if you pulled down the NFS, what would take its place? A whole series of private shops charging differing amounts for different types of food? Is that what Britainers really want? A complex and confusing network of big shops and some small ones. Some selling just fruit and veg (including pineapples. Pineapples? I don't even believe the fruit exists), others selling frozen food, and others prepared restaurant-style food. What next? Food brought to your door by a teenager on a bicycle?! Or organic vegetables delivered in boxes in a van? Ha ha. No, food is too important to be left up to individuals. The People of the United Isles deserve to be protected from the private food-stores who will simply exploit hungry people for money. And what about those who can't afford food. Are 'soup-kitchens' going to be opened up to give away food to the poor? Who can be relied upon for such counter-cultural kindness?'

Okay, now you can flush this book down the toilet.

Part Four: Academia, Science and all things Intellectual

'No man who worships education has got the best out of education ... Without a gentle contempt for education no man's education is complete.'

G. K. Chesterton

Our society is in awe of clever people. We love to marvel at people who understand things that are, to us, incomprehensible. Our TVs are full of 'experts'. Our news reports always contain reports of scientific papers. Perhaps the great boffin of our age is Stephen Fry. People love him because they think he's clever. Except he isn't really. He doesn't consider himself to be all that clever and will tell anyone who listens that he's merely been blessed with a phenomenal memory. This is probably true. People love Stephen Fry because he's lovely. And character is far more appealing than intelligence.

It is true that some of the greatest evils of the world have been perpetrated by the very intelligent. Many other evils have been carried out by those of average intellect but applauded by intellectuals and academics. Stalin is said to have called such people 'useful idiots'.

Governments always have a love-hate relationship with academia. They like to cite scientifically proven evidence to give weight to their policies (since they are utterly devoid of any compelling ideology). And Prime Ministers love to appoint tsars with specialised knowledge to sort things out. But sometimes the academics don't learn their place and go against policy as Professor David Nutt found when he had his own fact-based ideas about the classification of recreational drugs. And this is to say nothing of the tortuous relationship between science and religion.

Hence, this next section which is, I'll be honest, a bit of a rag bag. But in it we do consider all of the above by investigating greenhouse gases, World War Two, String theory, the God Particle and the reason for prime numbers being funnier than even ones.

String Theory and the God Particle

or: Why prime numbers are funny

As a professional comedy writer, take it from me that 37 is a funny number. If you look out for it in comedy, it appears far more frequently than most other two-digit numbers. When you're writing a script and you need an arbitrarily large number you'll probably reach for trusty 37, the Milton Keynes of numbers. Or you may chose 17, 23, 31, 53 or 71. Whichever you chose, your made-up number is likely to be odd, not even, and almost certainly prime.

There is another school of thought within younger comedy writers that rounder numbers are funnier. I don't believe it myself. 23 is funnier than 20, isn't it? But, maybe the Round Number Theory will gain widespread acceptance. Who knows?

I maintain that prime numbers are funny because they are a riddle in themselves. They bother, excite and annoy mathematicians. They are knots in the string of numbers. I once read a book on prime numbers by the brilliant Marcus du Sautoy. He did his best to explain it all in layman's terms, but it remains mostly baffling. But what I understand is most vexing about primes is the fact that they occur at completely unpredictable intervals. In a discipline where predictability is important, the irregularity of primes is enigmatic, tantalising and extremely irritating.

Similarly, physicists are still scratching their heads about how the universe fits together. There are two main branches of physics. One branch is about planets, gravity, forces and the big stuff; the Newtonian laws of physics with the Einstein upgrade. This branch is from the people that brought you 'dark matter', the indefinable stuff that you can't see, detect or measure, or even know about, but it's out there in universe somewhere, because if it isn't some of our equations don't work.

The other branch is quantum physics, the mechanics of the tiny. It's all about protons, photons and nutrinos (which until recently I thought was a yoghurt drink with bits of muesli). Quantum mechanics explains how to move faster than the speed of light and that sub-atomic particles can be in two places at once (although I don't know if they can give you eyes in the back of your head). It also teaches us that there are some things that are impossible for most people to understand, no matter how many BBC4-style documentaries you watch.

Put these two branches together and you have 'The Standard Model'. I don't know if there was an Authorised Model or New International Model, but there is an apparent need for a Revised Standard Model. The problem is that the two main branches of physics appear to be from slightly different trees. Clearly, they must all come from the same tree. And so physicists and mathematicians are seeking a 'theory of everything', which sounds like something from the mouth of Zaphod Beeblebrox.

The reason there's a very expensive particle accelerator called CERN is the quest to corroborate The Standard Model. They're searching for a particle called the Higgs Boson, popularly known as the God Particle. We shall return to this in a moment.

They also came up with string theory, which there seems little point in explaining. A version of it that is comprehensible and explainable in so few words will be so brief, facile and oversimplified that it will be meaningless. It would be like summing up Shakespeare's *Hamlet* by saying it's a play about 'this Danish bloke who gets a bit narked'.

What one can say is that string theory is a controversial theoretical multi-dimensional solution that is currently untested and untestable. In short, it's unscientific. Scientists often like to say that they are describing things as they are. They investigate, experiment, wait, measure, wait a bit more, measure again, write down, publish, wait and then realise that hardly anyone else in the world is interested in the Six-Spotted Green Tiger beetle, or the amount of nitrogen in the atmosphere of Neptune. But there seems to be no way of measuring, testing or proving string theory.

We're told that science is about observing facts and deriving conclusive theories; and that religion is about conclusive theories without any observable facts. Neither is true. Science is not about observing facts, but producing theories before looking for facts. Why do the mathematicians seek a Prime Number theory? Because they are convinced there must be a pattern to the seemingly endless prime numbers. They have faith in some unified theory of numbers, despite the evidence so far that there is no such theory. Likewise, why do the physicists pursue string theory? Because they are sure that there must be one theory to rule them all (and in the darkness bind them). If the universe is random, if cells just happened, if amino acids simply exist for no reason, why do scientists keep looking for ever more basic, simpler, grander explanations for everything? Why should there be a Standard Model at all? Why are we programmed for order and not chaos?

And yet, looking for meaning, and finding it in any kind of religion is often seen as fundamentally irrational. Terms like 'a leap of faith' crop up a lot these days. This all seems a bit rich given that a scientist is able to put forward string theory and explain that if it's true, there would be no way of gathering evidence for it. But many people seem to think that being a Christian is an exercise in self-delusion, making oneself believe things like the resurrection of Jesus Christ, which, of course, cannot possibly be true because dead people don't rise from the grave. In fact, believing something so scientifically implausible is so deluded some even consider it virtuous.

I first encountered this view in a conversation which takes place between Robbie Coltrane and Eric Idle in *Nuns on the*

Run twenty years ago. The former has to explain the Trinity to the latter. When Idle questions whether it makes sense, Coltrane says 'It doesn't make sense to anybody. That's why you have to believe it. That's why you need to have faith. If it made sense, it wouldn't be a religion would it?' He leans back and a picture from the wall falls onto his head. It's funny, but ultimately annoying because it doesn't describe my religious experience at all. Religion makes sense – or at least mine does.

The view that faith is irrational is now so commonplace that Christians are rarely portrayed on TV as anything other than credulous and naïve. The only alternative to the cretinously dumb is the hatefully arrogant type. And yet whenever either type of Christian is asked a difficult question on TV, they are shattered.

The credulous type, normally friendly young women, respond to questions in a way that implies that they have never heard these questions before and their faith is normally destroyed within five minutes; the latter furious type, normally older men, react by shutting down all questions and challenges by not listening and talking louder. This is how religion is discussed in the fictional land of television, where Christian characters tend not be measured, reasonable, good-humoured and intelligent all at the same time. And yet this describes most of the Christians I know.

I have written a play on the subject (called *The God Particle*). It is essentially the sort of play I would like to watch: two realistic people arguing about science and religion in an amusing and interesting way. And, unlike all other fictional discussions I'd seen, the religious character has actually given the matter some thought, listens to the arguments of other people and isn't devastated or livid when someone asks him about how a good God can allow suffering.

The ultimate question in the play revolves around what it is to have an open mind. Our society likes to portray scientists as open-minded, unemotional and swayed by nothing except carefully collected evidence. Religious people are typically closed-minded and unable to even consider new information or the viewpoints of others, when this is not my experience.

In recent years, I've been learning that I only say things that G. K. Chesterton said better than me more concisely a hundred years ago, hence the numerous quotations throughout this book. On this subject, he said: 'The purpose of having an open mind is the same as having an open mouth – to close it on something solid.' The question is whether it's ever right to close your mind on anything, no matter how solid. Our current age would say not.

Greenhouse Gases

or: Is it me or is it warm in here?
(Seriously, which is it?)

At school, I was hardly ever ill. I certainly avoided missing a whole day. It wasn't just good health, although I was pretty healthy as a child. I have hare-brained theories that it's something to do with exposure to dirt, being raised on a dairy farm and drinking unpasteurised milk.

I didn't like missing school because I hated having to play catch-up. If you missed a history lesson, and therefore the measures that Henry VII took to restore financial stability to England, you never really found out what they were. You may pick up a hand-out. You may even glance at someone else's notes, but you'd never bother to copy them out. You'd just not know about something permanently.

I feel like this with the climate change debate. Except I don't remember being ill. I can remember the early 1980s when there was talk of a new ice age. Then I was told that some scientists were thinking the world was actually getting warmer. Then suddenly, at some point on a day I can't remember, it switched. News reports stopped saying 'Scientists suspect that the world is warming.' They started saying 'We now know that the world is warming because of man-made CO_2'. Something changed. I missed the lesson. I don't really feel I've caught up, and I haven't been given the hand-out.

Please don't misunderstand me. I'm not a global-warming denier. You will already have discovered that I have strange, and bizarre opinions, but this is not one of them. I recycle. I love the idea of renewable energy. I'm excited about solar panels and the possibility of harnessing energy from sunlight. I take my own bags to the supermarket, even though it makes no difference to anything or anyone. And I watch *Top Gear* for the jokes and stunts, not the bioethics. But I missed the lesson in which someone convincingly explained to me, as an adult, how global warming actually works.

I had hoped that *An Inconvenient Truth* would fill in that gap. Sadly, it didn't. I saw graphs which showed correlation but not cause. There wasn't any convincing explanation. All the film really taught me is that Al Gore really likes Apple Mac computers, PowerPoint presentations and the sound of his own voice.

Now the debate has moved on, and I've been left behind. There is, apparently, broad scientific consensus, so if I don't understand it, it's my problem. I did wonder whether this was something I needed to understand for myself. I have no clue how my kidneys work, and I don't need to. But with global warming, I'm getting the sense that this is something I really should be able to grasp.

Instead, my lack of understanding and my questions now make it look like I'm in the camp of the naysayers, not a group I especially warm to. They are a bit of an odd bunch: Christopher Monckton, David Bellamy, Nigel Lawson and Johnny Ball. Whenever anyone asks a question about global warming, the campaigners tut and say 'The time for talking is over' and other fascistic statements designed to close down the debate in favour of expensive state intervention.

Besides, the time for talking is never over. Science is about talking. It's about questioning and challenging. It's about keeping an open mind. But the climate of fear around the climate debate is such that if I make negative comments about science in general, people will assume I'm a creationist lunatic with a house in the Nevada desert filled with canned goods.

But the awkward truth remains that general scientific consensus has been proved throughout history to be wrong. Almost all science is superseded by later science. Scientists often temporarily agree on things that turn out to be harmful, expensive, pointless, immoral or just plain wrong.

The other clod of mud often slung at global-warming sceptics is the one about vested interests. But to pretend that only the petrol heads have a vested interest is wilfully obtuse. Global warming is creating thousands of very comfortable jobs that involve gently pestering business (Yay! Stick it to the Man!), turning up to conferences in foreign cities, reading blogs, berating the public for not mulching and generally feeling good about yourself.

Imagine the surprise and disgust, then, when a recent survey revealed how many people in Britain today remain unconvinced about global warming, or humanity's part in it. It appeared that around half of those interviewed were sceptical or unsure.

All of this makes the church's desperation for relevance by talking about global warming – anything other than proper theology – all the more tragic, since it is clearly something that lots of people either don't understand, don't believe or are not interested in (which probably sums up their feelings about God too). I recently visited a cathedral where they clearly weren't all that sure about what Jesus' death on the cross actually meant, but they were very sure about the effect of greenhouse gases and how that should have an effect on your life.

Science has trends and fads. New theories gain ground and old theories die out. But the Church, which has had the same textbook – and God – for centuries, should really know better.

Halal Dolly

or: Why New Zealand Lamb is extra special

New Zealand is full of surprises. It's part Middle Earth and part Middle East, apparently. A newspaper not known for its broad-mindedness and tolerance recently reported that all lamb that comes from New Zealand is halal – that is, killed according to certain Islamic food regulations, including given a blessing. Given the newspaper's popularity, based on the knee-jerk xenophobia and Islamophobia across large parts of Britain, I assumed the story would be picked up and splashed across other newspapers. But it was not.

What are we to make of this? As a Christian, should I eat meat that has been offered to Allah? I don't believe that the God of the Bible and the God of Islam can really be the same, so would eating meat sacrifice to Allah make my God cross? Then I remembered St Paul's first letter to the Corinthians, chapter 10, especially after I looked up various words in a concordance. Paul says 'Eat whatever meat is sold in Tesco without raising any question on the grounds of conscience.' (N.B. some early manuscripts omit the words *Tesco* and read *meat market* or *Asda*.) In the rest of 1 Corinthians, and also Romans 14, Paul explains that if these things don't bother you, then they don't bother God, so tuck in. Tagines all round. But if it feels wrong, don't. And if others around you find this hard to stomach, refrain when you're around them and have the less exciting tagine with the apricots. (Paul was much more sensitive than some would have us believe.)

Given that supermarkets don't sell Holy Water, it seems odd that supermarkets would sell meat that had been killed in a certain way – a cruel way, in my opinion – and then dedicated to Allah 'the Most-Gracious, the Most Merciful' before being shrink-wrapped, frozen and labelled as merely 'New Zealand Lamb'.

Aside from whether Allah would like to be mentioned by name just above 'Cooking instructions' or 'Suitable for Home Freezing', I was concerned that the supermarkets were not being entirely straight with us. After all, livestock in Britain is carefully indexed and its movements and provenance dutifully catalogued. What about religious provenance, residual blessings and possible theological fall-out? So I decided to do some ground-breaking journalism, posing as a regular customer and, under the cover of darkness, wrote them an email.

Almost immediately, they replied, telling me that my email had been registered and would be answered 'as soon as possible'. I could tell my methods were rattling them because I heard nothing for an entire week. When I nudged them, I received two replies from two different people. The shorter was the more revealing, explaining that they complied with UK regulations and hadn't done anything illegal (known as the 'Fat Bankers Defence'). They also argued that extra labelling would cost more money that I, as a consumer, would have to pay. They realise that shuts most people up. They also assured me that the vast majority of their meat was produced on British farms without receiving the Halal blessing – and that their British Organic Lamb and their Willow Farm and Finest Chicken were certainly not Halal.

Food regulations require supermarkets to painstakingly list e-numbers, riboflavins and emulsifiers, display fat content (as a pie chart, ironically). It seems only fair that they should also mention whether or not the food was dedicated to a Supreme Being, whose legitimacy, identity, character or existence is questioned by at least half of the world's population. Presumably, they would also not need to tell us if the animal in question was once the property of White Supremacists, dedicated to Bunjil (aboriginal god of the Sky), or cloned in a lab just outside Edinburgh.

The second email added that some of their suppliers also supply Lamb to Muslim customers, but that all animals are properly stunned and feel no pain. Given the assurances of Food Standards Authority labelling regulations, the Apostle Paul and, most powerful of all, Tesco, is there really anything to worry about?

After all, even within Christianity, does blessing objects even work? Numerous church traditions can become vexed about consecrated things in a way that doesn't seem to chime with the New Testament. As a whole, the Bible doesn't go in for magic swords and talismans of invincibility (more's the pity, some would say). Moses' staff wasn't magic. You couldn't steal it and part rivers with it. Granted, the Ark of the Covenant was deadly, but as a rule all power and blessing comes from God, not blessed or spiritually supercharged objects. Ceremonial items, like wafers, wine and water are consumable and do not last – like the manna in the desert so that God's people would depend on Him for their daily bread.

So should I eat Halal lamb? Fortunately, I'm spared the dilemma. Lamb – holy, Halal or British organic – is just too expensive.

Move Over, Darling

or: Would the last member of the human race please turn out the lights?

With every week that passes, one stumbles across yet another reason why Professor Dawkins is wrong. Here's my latest discovery. The humble *homo sapiens* is the only 'animal' that thinks the world would be better off without it. We are like the lemmings who famously throw themselves off cliffs. Although the film that captured mass lemming suicide was almost as famously contrived and in no way scientific. But the fact remains; we think we should delete ourselves from existence because we are violent, greedy and wasteful. We extinguish other species, we chop down trees, and then leave our litter where the tree should have been. How would Professor Dawkins explain this anti-evolutionary urge to see one's DNA RIP?

Where is the evidence for this urge, I hear you cry. Exhibit A: Corinne Maier, a French writer, who penned a book entitled *No Kid: 40 Reasons Not to Have Children* (except in French). She doesn't seem to be joking when she produces forty compelling arguments which include arguing that children are expensive, stop you having fun and turn you into an idiot as you attempt to communicate with them. Plus you can't stop yourself from wanting your children to be happy so you'll be forced into being their slave.

The book sounds like it's written by a thirteen year-old boy, but Maier is in fact a mother of two, deeply regretted children. They must be the only children in the world who, when on television for the first time do not say 'Hello, Mum'. Nonetheless, she urges 'my brothers and sisters in arms, stay disunited, sceptical and, if possible, without descendants'.

She is not a one-off. A year before this book emerged, Alan Weisman published a book called *The World Without Us* in which he examined how a post-apocalyptic world would regenerate. Also, in 1991, a man called Les U. Knight formed a group called VHEMT (pronounced 'vehement'), which stands for the Voluntary Human Extinction MovemenT. Their motto is 'May we live long and die out'. He means it. Many may laugh, but not as hard as they would have done some years ago. In 1998, Bill McKibben was largely derided when he wrote a book called *Maybe One* based on his giving up the second child he wanted to have a vasectomy instead in order to prevent global warming.

There have always been worries about population. Paul Ehrlich terrified the world with his book *The Population Bomb* in 1968. In it, he cheerfully stated 'The battle to feed all of humanity is over. In the 1970s and 1980s hundreds of millions of people will starve to death in spite of any crash programs embarked upon now.' Who can blame him? Scaring the living daylights out of people is a long and noble tradition. It is also tremendous fun. You get to go on the TV a lot – there's always a slot for you on one of the rolling news channels. People will buy your book. And some people, albeit fewer, will buy your follow-up book twenty years later saying why you were still right, theoretically; just not in practice.

But population concerns have moved beyond arguments about scarcity of food and resources. It has been become a moral argument. Self-immolating westerners are beginning to agree with Corinne Maier when she writes 'To have a child in Europe or America is immoral – more scarce resources wasted on a way of life that is ever more voracious, capricious, hungry for fuel and destructive of the environment.'

By the gates of schools in West London, turning up with five children would certainly be frowned upon, partly for environmental reasons. Westerners really are increasingly convincing themselves that large families are not just demanding and expensive, but morally bad.

However, family planning, or curbing, is already starting to unravel all over the world. The Chinese are worried about 'Little Emperor Syndrome'. They have a generation of children who are their parents' only child. These children are used to having everything money can buy – and in some cases are being over-nourished by grandparents starved of grandchildren to force-feed sweets. Many of these children would surely have benefited from being in a family with brother and sisters, learning to share, to listen and get their siblings into trouble while their mum's back was turned?

In other countries, politicians are more worried about the lack of babies. The Japanese tremble at the thought of who is going to pay their pensions. The French have bribed their citizens to have a third child with bonus benefits and a lump sum. Russia, covering a seventh of the Earth's land, has only 141 million citizens, making it very sparsely populated in the global league tables. So in places like Ulyanovsk on the Volga, parents are encouraged to 'give birth to a patriot'. If you successfully conceive on Conception day, nine months later you could win a truck – leading to all sorts of amusing rhyming slogans (which work less well in Russian).

Despite the hand-wringing of guilty westerners, many people around the world know that large families are a good thing. In the Bible, Abraham was promised many descendants – as numerous as stars in the sky. This was meant to be a blessing, not a recipe for an environmental nightmare. If we need to adapt our habits to make room for others, that too is a blessing. The idea that the world would be better off without us is simply not true. Genesis shows us that God has made nature abundant, fruitful and in need of human management.

Beside, once we're gone, who would appreciate the beauty of the world left behind? If environmental extinctionists do lay down their lives, they will be leaving it to the very people they despise: gas-guzzling, gun-toting right-wing fundamentalist American families with 15 kids, four of them called Enos (one of whom is a girl). So it might be more productive to learn to live with each other.

The Appeal of World War Two

or: Why Hitler makes such great television

It was typical of the fortunes of English cricket that its long-awaited buoyancy should have coincided with its vanishing from our terrestrial televisions. After the amazing Ashes series of 2005, the rights to Test Match Cricket were gobbled up by Sky. Hence, Rupert Murdoch has been receiving regular payments from me so that I have been able to watch England's rise to be world number 1, before a slow decline. All for twenty pounds a month.

All of this means that with Sky and Freeview, I am now able to watch a documentary about World War Two at any moment. Why are there so many?

There is an obvious reason for this, at least in media terms. Footage of the war is either cheap or free; and there are still plenty of war veterans and survivors available to talk about their experiences. These interviews can be very difficult to listen to and watch as you spend most of the time trying to work out how old they are before deciding whether or not they look good for their age. Usually they look fabulous, although that in itself does not lend credence to theory of the old buffer who always says that 'what this country needs is a war'. We've had one in Iraq and still have one in Afghanistan. I don't think it's helping.

Clearly the programmes about World War Two are sufficiently popular to justify even their comparatively small expense. The fact is, they demonstrate that, as a nation, we are still obsessed with World War Two. Every year brings a new anniversary commemorating everything that took place from the invasion of Poland in 1939 until the fall of Berlin in 1945. Video stores are filled with films of the war; bookshelves groan under the weight of words written about it; and nine-year-olds are rarely happier than when they're clearing a German machine-gun nest with their X Box.

Perhaps the appeal is that, as Britons, we flatter ourselves that it was we who really vanquished the fascist, fanatical Axis powers. The way that the war is traditionally portrayed in Britain, one would have no reason to suspect that is not the case. There are many moving and self-aggrandising films in the canon (if you'll pardon the pun), but *A Bridge Too Far*, and all-star movie about Allied failure in Holland in 1944, hardly balances things up.

Britain does indeed deserve credit for defiantly standing alone in the early years of the war, but when it came to expending human lives, the vast brunt of the casualties were taken by Russia, who lost tens of millions of their number. And in Normandy and into Germany, the Brits were increasingly outnumbered by the Americans who poured thousands more troops into Europe than into the Pacific to fight Japan.

Jingoism aside, the appeal of the war could be in the leaders; not in their actions, but in their apparent comic-book simplicity. Characters like Churchill, with his cigar, Montgomery, with his implausibly large beret, and Patton, with his Yosemite Sam spirit, would be criticised as clichés were they to be invented and portrayed on a big screen. The same could be said of Hitler, who has been a reference point of evil for over seventy years. Hitler's invasion of country after country in the early 1940s demonstrated that his conduct of international politics was more akin to a game of *Risk*. In a similar fashion, Churchill, Stalin and Roosevelt decided the fates of entire continents on scraps of paper passed across tables, bargaining with countries like betting chips. You can almost imagine Stalin saying, 'I see your Moldova and I'll raise you a Ukraine.'

Stalin is equally exaggerated in personal traits, a carica-
ture of evil, directly responsible for even more deaths than
Hitler. But Stalin is the uncomfortable figure who reminds
us that World War Two was not the simple struggle of good
versus evil. The war has been, and frequently still is, painted
as a simple struggle between the honest Tommy and the
vile, unredeemable Nazi. Even in Normandy, this generali-
sation won't do, as, by 1944, the German army contained
thousands of conscripts from all over Europe who were no
more Nazi than the Pope (bad example?).

Moreover, Russian troops, like Nazi troops, committed
numerous acts of appalling atrocity whilst wearing
American-made boots, and driving Uncle Sam's trucks.
Keeping Russian troops supplied undoubtedly saved hundreds of thousands of American casualties which would
otherwise have been sustained in France and Flanders, but
at what cost to the Czechs, the Latvians and, ultimately, the
Poles, over whom Britain valiantly went to war, and were in
turn surrendered to the Soviets for fifty years? This moral
ambiguity in itself is part of the attraction of the war.

But more fascinating than the compromises made
between good and evil, perhaps, is the evil itself. As
humans, not only are we unpleasant, we find the whole
history and science of unpleasantness utterly absorbing.
Anthony Beevor's highly-acclaimed classics, *Stalingrad* and
Berlin, along with any history of the war in the East or the
Far East are littered with tales of ruthlessness, depravity and
woe.

One could argue that the war demonstrated the strength
of the human spirit in spite of such immense suffering.
Tolerance of the likes of Hitler would never be accepted
now, surely? The mass graves in the former Yugoslavia and
Rwanda would suggest we are excellent at tolerating evil
and slaughter.

A quick flick through the Bible teaches what we know to
be true – humans don't change. We are 'senseless, faithless,
heartless and ruthless' (Romans 1:31). One thing the war did
demonstrate was how easily we live with, and can be drawn
into, acts of grotesque evil. Every reader of these stories, or

viewer of *Nazis: A Warning from History*, wonders how they would have reacted in the circumstances. The prognosis is not flattering. We are not the heroes we would like to think we are.

Part Five: Church, Religion and all things Spiritual

'The first effect of not believing in God is to believe in anything.'
Émile Cammaerts
The Laughing Prophet

So, we have looked at The Media, The City, The State, and Academia. And we now turn to The Church. This is the point at which one might expect many readers to give up in favour of that Malcolm Gladwell book about some abstract noun that you bought on a whim on Amazon months ago and still haven't got round to reading. Fair enough.

But before you put me down, I want you to know that I sympathise with your lack of interest. After all, the Church is a widely discredited and disgraced organisation – in fact it is not even one organisation but a loose federation of warring tribes based on the teaching of a man who seemed to be all about peace, which doesn't seem right. What could the Church possibly have to offer our civilisation, beyond a fuzzy sense of hope or some old buildings that could be turned into flats and sold for some good money?

Many see the decline of religion as both a good thing and a merciful inevitability. If I searched the internet for a few moments, I'm sure I would find some vitriolic quotations from Richard Dawkins on the subject but let's keep the mood light, shall we? The fact remains the abuses of the church in the past and present are, sadly, all too obvious. And yet, flawed and fragmented, the church offers solutions on how to mend this society that has been ruined by civilisation.

As a society, we have rejected the church. But every rejection is a choice. Not just a choice to go without something, but a choice to replace it with something else. Smoking is an anti-social habit. If you give up smoking, you will find other things to do with your hands and mouth. If those things are eating unhealthy amounts of fatty food, you may be better off smoking. Something is clearly awry when the cure is not only worse than the disease but deadly.

If we have given up on philosophy, religion and church, we need to examine what we have replaced them with – movies, money, politics and pills. Those things are the four institutions we've just been considering: The Media, The City, The State, and Academia. I'm not saying these institutions are the Four Horsemen of the Apocalypse. Not at all. These things are all good things and have their place. But to make a better society, media, money, law and science are useful allies, but poor masters.

The question we're all trying to answer is how do you make society better, kinder and more content? The hopes of today rest on our widely despised politicians to pass laws that will make us play nicely. The problem is that the State has a monopoly on legal violence and its laws are ultimately enforced at gun point. Law is not a subtle instrument. Therefore anyone who breaks the law which states 'Thou Shalt Not say things that make thy neighbour feel bad' has to be punished. If you tweet or blog something antisocial and break the current batch of daft laws on what is permissible, they will come to your house with guns and take you away. Is that really what we want?

The hopes of today rest on employment, 'getting Britain back to work' and raising the standard of living. A laudable aim, but money is not the solution. We cannot simply pay people to do the right thing and make the country a better place. Money talks. But it frequently lies. We've just been learning that lesson again the hard way.

Scientists are busy finding cures for our woes – and cures and vaccinations for global scourges like AIDS and malaria will undoubtedly do great good. But medicine makes life possible – it doesn't make life worth living. And if all of the above is too depressing, put on a movie. Or watch all ten seasons of *Friends*. It really will make you feel better. But only for a while.

What is left? However implausible it may seem, perhaps the church merits another look. As always, G. K. Chesterton put it better. In *What's Wrong with the World* (1910) he wrote: 'The Christian ideal has not been tried and found wanting. It has been found difficult; and left untried.' Maybe the church can deliver a hope that's outside of ourselves, a contentment based on something shared, rather than something selfish – a society saved rather than self-improved. Speaking of which, let us begin by thinking about Christmas ...

Christian Festivals, Part 1: Christmas

or: The best fit for the facts

A few years ago, Ricky Gervais wrote a pleasant and personal Holiday Message – partly explaining his atheism. In it, he respectfully argues that his atheism stems from childhood when he couldn't help but feel that his belief in God was a lie. And that he had been lied to. It's interesting that he abandoned his faith because of an experience. When his faith was challenged, he didn't seek proof or evidence, but gave up hope in the possibility of a god. In the same article, Gervais also says that science dispassionately seeks out the truth and bases its conclusions on concrete evidence whereas believing in something doesn't make it true.

This is a popular and widespread view – that science is definitive and factual and that religion is purely sensory and imaginary. This may be true of some faiths and spiritualities which make no claim to have any factual or scientific basis. But it puzzles me that many people still make this charge against Christianity, which is, to some extent, sensory, but it is also factual.

As chronically un-romantic as it seems, the 'factualness' of Christianity is the very thing we celebrate at Christmas – Jesus as God Incarnate, that is to say God born on earth, as a baby, made of the same flesh and bone as you or me. It's why Jesus is called 'Emmanuel' in some of the birth narratives, because it means 'God with us'. Christianity does not worship a distant, silent God who is unknown and unknowable, unless we've been thoroughly beguiled by some silly Dan Brown, whose theories have no credence within even the most anti-Christians circles of academia. No one is seriously contesting the existence of the man, Jesus of Nazareth, who lived for 30-odd years before dying on a cross.

And if this Jesus had lived a dull, uneventful life and died at the age of 70 and was buried, the claim that Jesus was God would undoubtedly have less credence. But his short life was far from uneventful. He performed miracles to a sceptical crowd. He taught strangers how to live in ways which astonished them. Without writing a single book, composing a single song or holding a single position of earthly authority, he became the most notorious, intriguing man in all of human history.

Now, if we're being open-mindedly scientific, surely we need to take a look at the facts again? To say they are invented is to prejudge them. To insist that his miracles can't have happened is to discriminate against them. To assume the people of the time were easily fooled is a judgment that requires evidence.

Followers of Jesus Christ aren't suggesting for a moment that simply anyone can heal the sick, walk on water or raise the dead. But they are insisting that one man can. Christians don't have faith in this because they are trying to convince themselves it's true in spite of the facts. They are saying that Jesus' claim to be God himself is the best fit for the facts.

Maybe, this Christmas, we could be more like the good scientists who take one more look at the facts. The results may be surprising.

Religion and Offence, Part 1: Jesus, the Early Years

or: How to publicise a one-man Fringe show for free

In the month of August, Edinburgh is a city under siege. Most of the assailants are English – a mixture of penniless young comedians or actors clinging together in sketch groups for safety. Then there are the techies, the agents, producers, talent scouts and the PR people, promoting the aforementioned young actors and comedians (and are themselves the reason for the young actors' pennilessness). Add to that the International Festival, the Book Festival, the TV Festival and The Edinburgh Military Tattoo and you have one month of total bedlam.

Bloated and out of control, the world's largest festival continues year after year. And every couple of years, the Fringe normally belches out some proper old fashioned blasphemy – normally a controversial depiction of Christ on stage. The media are normally grateful for this, August being traditionally a slow month. When it does happen again, as it surely will, it will probably unfold along the following lines:

An unknown comedian, Jonny Clever, announces his new Edinburgh comedy show: *Jesus: The Early Years*. In it, Jonny Clever plays the part of Jesus in a coming-of-age comedy about Jesus of Nazareth's tricky teens, in which he works for his father's carpentry business, bunks off, and drinks too much water that he changes into wine. He swears and chases girls before discovering he'd have an easier life and be more attractive to women giving talks about peace and love than making furniture. There are simulated sex acts and it's all a bit tawdry, but eventually, after getting his material right, he is set on the trajectory we read about in the Bible. So far, so blasphemous.

Jonny Clever sends out his press releases in July or gets his girlfriend who works in PR to do it. Almost all of them are ignored, except for one journalist, Sally Hack, on one national newspaper, who can't think of anything else to write. She picks up the press release off the 'free stories' pile and this one is a no-brainer as she has the mobile number of a couple of angry Christians. A few calls and Sally Hack will be able to say that 'Christian groups are up arms' about the show. Which they aren't. Or weren't until they heard about it. But some of them will be by the time they've read the piece they're writing.

Other church leaders are informed. Some shrug. They are ignored. Some are offended. They are invited on to a few radio talk shows. The show starts the Edinburgh run. It does quite well. Because it's quite funny. Witty in places. Some standard jokes about mass-catering, loaves and fish. A funny flashback to the stable and a genuinely original routine about the Three Wise Men. There are also a few shockingly offensive gags, some of which delight the audience, others of which do not.

Reviews are plentiful but mixed. No award nominations, but it achieves sufficient notoriety to be offered a limited run in an Off-West End theatre. Jonny Clever steps down from the role, as he isn't a particularly good actor. Tommy Sharp, the successful comedian and writer sharpens up the script. And Harry Hansom-Famous, American film actor, steps in to the title role. It moves to a larger West End theatre which is, in turn, picketed by a handful of Christians.

For one day and night, another round of radio phone-in shows discusses the merits of the show. The arguments advanced by various Christian speakers, vicars and pastors on the networks are 'that faith is very personal and it's not right that it's lampooned in this way'. Also 'Jesus died for sinners and lived a perfect life. This play is misleading people and humiliating the saviour of the World.' Others say 'This so-called comedy marks the final nail in the coffin of our so-called Christian society with proper respect for authority'. Secular commentators say, 'We don't live in a Christian society and haven't done for years'. Secular comedians say, 'Comedians need to be able to say the unsayable. It's free speech.' Others say 'Christians should be able to take a joke. After all, if their God is real, he doesn't need us to fight his battles'.

The debate crawls into a second day. A few traditional bishops are officially 'saddened'. A few trendy bishops 'welcome the opportunity to debate Jesus' life'. A few theologians give a scriptural basis for the play based on The Gospel of Bartholomew (which they date to around 150AD) which details early philandering on the part of Jesus (at least the fragments do if you fill in enough of the blanks). Other theologians say the gospels date to 350AD.

Then some Christians say 'These comedians wouldn't criticise Islam or Mohammed like this.' And everyone agrees but no one knows what to do about that. And it's all over before someone can point out that we can't criticise Islam in the same way as Christianity because there aren't enough shared reference points or cultural understanding for comedy about Islam to appear anything other than vindictive or hateful. But by this time, the West End run ends after eight weeks. And everyone waits for the same sort of thing to happen again some time soon.

Life, Liberty and the Pursuit of Happiness

or: The myth of common decency

The year is 597 AD – the headline of the *Canterbury Chronicle* is '40 Monks Drown At Sea.' Pope Gregory's mission to England is a disastrous failure. Roman Christianity fails to arrive in Britain and Celtic Christianity dies out – since its most fervent adherents insist on living in chaste isolation. Britain remains firmly pagan.

A druidic revival ensues, reasserting nature-based, solar-inspired theology. Stonehenge becomes an ancient, holy centre of worship. A city builds up around the holy place. The odd virgin is sacrificed on special days. The Vikings arrive and depart – throwing some Norse gods into the mix. Druidic teaching incorporates Thor, Woden and Freya. The occasional baby is ritually burned to appease the pantheon of gods.

Then, in 1066, William of Normandy takes one look at England and really doesn't fancy it. The Normans never arrive. A few hundred years later, the Spanish mount a spirited crusade against these odd animistic savages called Britons but are quickly repulsed by the unexpected violence and barbarism of the primitive painted warriors.

Britain is a truly wild and bizarre island. They do not worship a Triune God or respect learning; even trade and commerce is treated with suspicion. Druidic teaching at the time demands that all the sick and dying be expelled from the community; the poor are viewed with suspicion since they have clearly angered the gods in some way. A few hundred years later, in 2007, Britain is a poor and pitied country. Druid priests rule, chickens are held to be holy, and their eggs sacred. Polygamy is widespread and the age of consent is eleven. In many ways, it resembles some societies on the Pacific Rim.

Now, it's worth asking the question: Why is Britain not like this? Here's one reason. The boat containing those forty monks did not sink. It's probably not the *only* reason, but Britain did become a Christian nation. Christianity soaked through into the psyche of the British people – which is why Britons don't have the same values as the people of Papua New Guinea or Saudi Arabia. This seems obvious, and yet strident atheists seem unable to grasp this simple idea.

With every furious book Professor Richard Dawkins publishes, atheism acquires more self-confidence; almost a swagger. Over the years, he has been joined by Christopher Hitchens with his *God Is Not Great: The Case Against Religion* and John Gray with *Black Mass: Apocalyptic Religion and the Death of Utopia* to name but a few. Other voices include Philip Pullman, Polly Toynbee and Jonathan Miller. The secular choir gets louder every year.

The nihilists know what they're doing. Ironically, they have it all planned out, despite claiming that it's religion that is all about control. They're spreading the gospel of nothingness; preaching that the god-shaped hole in our hearts is just a hole that's not yet been closed up by evolution, chromosomes or memes. They constantly insist that religion is not only harmful ('Religion poisons everything', claimed Hitchens), but completely unnecessary. Who needs religion, they claim, when we can get by with good old common decency?

The problem with ardent atheists is that their quest to put some kind of social order in place ends up appealing to universal professions and declarations of rights. The early inspiration is the American Bill of Rights in which the authors 'hold these truths to be self-evident, that all men are created equal, that they are endowed, by their Creator (ignore that bit, obviously), with certain unalienable Rights, that among these are Life, Liberty, and the pursuit of Happiness.'

Surely we can agree that these rights are unalienable and self-evident? No. The only reason any of the Rights in the Bill were self-evident to the authors of the document was because they were, by and large, Christians. Moreover, their forefathers were evangelical dissidents. Are these truths self-evident to people in Yemen?

What about Universal Declaration of Human Rights? Are they really self-evident? Article 1 asserts that all human beings are born free and equal in dignity and rights. So what about the Indian caste system? Article 6 declares everyone has the right to recognition everywhere as a person before the law. This is not self-evident in Pakistan, where the testimony of women is marginalised in court. Article 9 says that no one shall be subjected to arbitrary arrest, detention or exile. Arbitrary arrest seems to be sensible for the people in authority in China or other oppressive regimes. Article 16 is about the right to marry at a 'full age'. What age is that? In Britain it is 16. In other countries, that is not the case – and they seem happy with that. And can we agree on polygamy? The article also says that 'the family is the natural and fundamental group unit of society and is entitled to protection by society and the State'. To some in the west, this is offensive and wrong – including, apparently, to many of our own politicians.

Western social norms and mores are far from universal. In fact, many 'self-evident truths' are utterly offensive to 'civilised' people from other nations. Let's not kid ourselves there's a self-evident DNA-proof human code of common acceptable behaviour. It's a nonsense. It doesn't exist. What's the inherent self-evident worth of a walking bag of blood and bones? Nothing, surely? How can a DNA-propagating animal work out a private morality, let alone a public one?

The fact is that Dawkins, Toynbee and Pullman all enjoy the benefits of a Christian society, which includes freedom of expression, equality before the law and tolerance – a

Christian virtue that, admittedly, many Christians have been hazy on. In many parts of the world, Toynbee would have been denied a career on account of her sex. Pullman would have been put in prison for his beliefs.Dawkins would have been excluded from academia. They should be grateful that Augustine's boat arrived with the good news about Jesus Christ.

Metropolis

or: How living in cities makes you a nicer person

Every few years, London elects a new mayor. In most normal, British elections, feverish counting begins as soon as the polls close at 10 pm on Thursday. But in London mayoral elections, the counting begins at a leisurely 8.30 am on Friday morning, after a light breakfast of coffee and bagels. The winner is announced later that day so that the first thing the winning candidate can do in office is take a well-deserved weekend off, ideally in the country and away from the ghastly city that has to be governed.

The reality is that, with the exception of the young and hip, most people wince at the thought of a large city. The word 'urban' is associated with other words like 'crime', 'poverty' and 'deprivation'. Urban culture invokes images of jagged writing on concrete walls, spray paint, uncollected rubbish and an excessive use of the letter 'z'. 'Inner-cities' sound uniformly gloomy and without hope. So it's no surprise that many of us who live in cities plan to leave at some point in the future to pursue a life of middle-class surburban ennui or rustic simplicity – as your author has in fact already done, having lived in London for nearly 15 years.

It is common to assume that Christianity is a religion of the countryside. J. R. R. Tolkein's shires and C. S. Lewis's Narnia both promote living alongside nature and streams, rather than flyovers and municipal swimming baths. In Genesis, God made the mountains and the hills, plants, birds, animals and fish.

Moreover, many people, including lots of Christians, think that heaven is a regression to Eden; that Christians can look forward to some kind of Hawaiian, leafy paradise in which trees abound in permanently ripe fruit and it's always warm. Except I don't really like fruit. I can be talked into eating bananas but in heaven, I'd like bacon. And I don't want sit around in gardens for ever – although if I die aged 71 and remain that age permanently in heaven, I probably will want to sit around in gardens for ever.

But this just underlines how we've taken thoughts of heaven from pop-culture and Plato, rather than the Bible. The Bible starts in a garden in Genesis and ends in a city in Revelation, giving us a clear idea of what heaven will be like. It is not a Nirvana-like state of permanent bliss in which we float around as disembodied spirits in some ethereal soup. Heaven is a lobby for the New Heavens and New Earth, which contain a vast shining city, the New Jerusalem. Who'd've thunk it? The afterlife is a city. (And I'm still reeling from the revelation that God is a DJ.)

But this city is not just a sprawling metropolis of tower-blocks. A river runs through it and a tree grows with leaves that will heal the nations. It's a garden city. Could it be that Welwyn Garden City is simply way ahead of its time?

This is all hard to swallow in the Bible, where cities tend to be places where bad things happen. Look at Babel, where men got together and decided to build a tower to God. Look at Sodom and Gomorrah where men just got together. Look at Nineveh, the hated city that inspired Jonah to sail in the opposite direction as fast as he could.

But cities are only sinful places because they're great gatherings of sinners. And that's why God loves cities. Jonah wanted God to zap Nineveh out of existence and sat on his hill eating popcorn waiting for it to happen. But God tells Jonah that Nineveh is full of thousands of people who cannot tell their right hand from their left (which explains why it took three days to cross the city. It must have been gridlocked if people couldn't tell apart left and right). But the final words of the book of Jonah are God saying, 'Should I not be concerned about that great city?' (Jonah 4:11).

So whoever runs London, New York, Moscow, Rotterdam or anywhere, they can be encouraged that God loves cities. But how do you run one? Cities, like God, operate on grace which is 'cheerfully putting up with stuff you don't like'. (Apologies if I'm getting too technical.) In cities, your garden isn't as big as you'd like, and it's next to someone else's whose tree scatters leaves on your lawn. And upstairs is a family with kids who stomp around and use their washing machine at 2 am And you can't park outside your house. Especially on match day. You need grace to live in a city and anything that teaches us grace is a Good Thing.

How to Watch Television

or: One of the main causes of Christians being holier-than-thou

I don't read as many Christian books as I should. Hardly anyone does. But a while ago I read one that has advised me to throw away my television. After all, who really needs a television? It's just a 32-inch 24-hour mind pollutant continually thrusting godless images of into your head. BBC1 and ITV worship at the idol of celebrity, while BBC2, Channel 4 and Five keep churning out food porn, property porn, and actual porn. And on cable it's more of the same plus sport, films, reruns and entire days of documentaries about Hitler.

One can see the logic. As an Evangelical, I understand the emphasis on personal holiness and godliness and not filling your mind with images and stories that encourage lust, greed, envy and rage (and that's just *EastEnders*).

Of course, no one actually needs a television like they need heat, light, clothing, food and water, but some of us actually like watching television and consider access to *The Great British Bake Off* a basic human right. We also have children, so a television is very handy (plus the BBC licence fee is worth it for CBeebies alone). Moreover, I work in television so living without one isn't exactly practical. I don't want to be one of those irritatingly aloof people in the media who work in TV but don't actually own one. They do exist. I am not on their team.

Therefore, as a scriptwriter of television programmes and therefore ludicrously biased, I would like to mount a defence of television and suggest ways of operating with at least one in the house.

Because I work in television, I'll begin by playing dirty and attacking the opposition. Those who advocate ditching the television often say 'There's never anything on television anyway'. This, of course, presupposes that a broadcaster should be broadcasting exactly the programme you want to watch at exactly the time you want to watch it. Granted, there is a lot of terrible television – practically anything broadcast before 6 pm, but don't forget the same machine that churns out *Jeremy Kyle* and *The Only Way is Essex* also gives you *Downton Abbey*, *Modern Family,* and David Attenborough documentaries. And bear in mind, that some TV isn't meant to moving wallpaper but is intended be uncomfortable and visceral because it's making a point, satirising, showing the world how it is, rather than the world as we'd like it to be.

Has TV got worse? Was it all cleaner, more wholesome, and funnier back in the days when there were just three channels? (N.B.: To readers under the age of 35, you need to know that in 1980, there were only three TV channels. And they didn't even broadcast through the night). The golden era of television is something of a myth. We may remember Morecambe and Wise, but we've forgotten about a whole host of programmes that were just lousy. But, secondly, are things getting morally worse in terms of content? Possibly. The worst stuff now is definitely worse than the stuff of yesteryear. Dozens of programmes on today would have been unthinkable twenty years ago. On the other hand, the unequivocally racist sit-com from the seventies *Love thy Neighbour* wouldn't be even be pitched to a TV Commissioner. And, *Blue Peter* is still going.

So, here's how to keep a television in the house without it causing unsightly stains on your brain.

Channel hopping is fatal – Not only does it infuriate the lady of the house, or anyone else forbidden from touching the remote control, it's impossible to tell if a programme is any good by watching it for twenty seconds and making a snap decision. Someone has probably put together a programme to be watched as a whole, so this is a bad way of finding a good TV show, but it is very tempting to just get in and switch on the television. There may be a reason for this:

Change your living room layout – it shouldn't be any surprise that if we have a television in the living room, we are instinctively drawn to it because, more often than not, our whole living room layout points at the television. It sits in the corner like a shrine and every available seat, sofa and easy-chair is expectantly looking at it. Move things around so not everything is facing the screen. I know some people who keep the TV in cupboard. This is a little extreme but worth considering.

Do not even turn on the television before consulting a TV guide – Once the TV is on, the colours begin to dance on the screen, and before you know it, you've watched half an hour of *Celebrity Dentists' Weakest Link*. And then the channel hopping starts and you look at your watch, two hours have evaporated and it doesn't feel like you've watched anything. Normally, there isn't anything on of any interest exactly when you want it to be, so don't switch on the telly on the off-chance. Plan your viewing.

Get a good TV guide – The *Radio Times* has been available since about 1937. It is Britain's bestselling magazine. Despite the name of the magazine, it contains long lists of programmes that are on television along with the times that they are on. Have a look. You will find a few things worth watching. And just before they're on, switch on the TV. When they have finished, switch the TV off. Beware of some TV guides which seem to be just a way of selling multi-coloured paper. A good TV guide is invaluable and will tell you when a programme isn't half as interesting as it sounds, or much more helpful and interesting than it looks (e.g. *Wife Swap* and *Desperate Housewives* were both actually much better than they sounded).

Work out how to use your video recorder/PVR/Sky Plus – We've established that channel hopping is bad and TV guides are good. Now, if you're an Evangelical, you are probably the sort of person who is trying but failing to cut down on the number of Christian meetings you go to. So you're never in when the good stuff is on. Solution? Use your Video Recorder, or Freeview Hard Drive. It's really not that hard. If you can operate a mobile phone, you really can programme a video recorder if you can be bothered. Tape the good stuff. And watch at your convenience.

If you think a programme is morally reprehensible, tell them – The fact is in today's post-Judeo-Christian society, TV commissioners, controllers and regulators don't really know what is acceptable and what isn't. But the thing that gets them rattled is complaints. When was the last time you actually contacted the BBC to complain about a particular programme? They have to take complaints seriously. The broadcasting laws and statutes say so. Many thoroughly dreadful or godless programmes go for weeks and weeks without getting complaints. How are the commissioners meant to know it's offending people if nobody tells them? If you feel a programme has overstepped the mark of taste and decency, pick up the phone, send an email or even write a letter.

If you think a programme is good, tell them – Why should just Christians be the unrelenting complainers? TV execs and producers think religious folk are just prudish whingers or, even worse, hypocrites. Mary Whitehouse, well-meaning as she was, gave the impression that she watched TV with a note-pad simply waiting to be shocked whilst keeping score of the swear words. Do you have a favourite programme? Then why not write to the BBC and tell them? Email them. Dozens of phone calls and emails in praise of programmes gets them re-commissioned. The viewers are not powerless.

So, before you throw your television into a skip with smug satisfaction, consider whether you've actually been fair to your poor Panasonic. Sure, it often shows you the wrong programme at the wrong time, but with a bit of skilful manoeuvring, you could find a decent hour of television every day. And it'll do you no more harm than reading any given national newspaper which is stuffed full of its own inaccuracies and prejudices. Enjoy. (It is allowed.)

Christian Festivals, Part 2: Lent

or: Why giving things up is chronically over-rated

Let us be clear about this. Giving up chocolate for Lent isn't a thing. I can't claim to understand Lent. I'm a Calvinist so I live like it's Lent all year round. It's taken me years to convince myself that I'm allowed a large glass of orange juice and that it's not the luxury item (like it was in the 1980s when it was considered to be a starter in a three course meal). So I may not be confident on the provenance of Lent. But I do know this. Whatever it's about, it's not about giving up chocolate for forty days.

Here's what I do know: Lent traditionally begins on Ash Wednesday, the day after the Sacred Feast of the Pancakes, and ends on Maundy Thursday (a.k.a. The Day of Worrying about What Time to Leave the Next Day to Beat the Traffic on the A303).

Most Christian festivals, feast days and oddities are based on something biblical that is worth of being remembered and celebrated (although the practice of Beating the Bounds is just plain weird). Lent has closer ties to the Bible than most. The period is obviously linked to Jesus being tempted in the Wilderness for forty days and forty nights. This is, in turn, linked with the Israelites wandering in the Wilderness for forty years. The former is about faithfulness and fasting, the latter is about faithlessness and getting bored of the same dinner. (I like quail as much as the next man, but I wouldn't want it every day.)

Why this forty day period has been earmarked as the 'pre-match build-up' to Easter is less clear to me. But it has been a tradition in numerous Christian denominations for centuries. Ironically, it seems to be one of the few things they have in common.

Lent seems to be about fasting. But what does Jesus make of fasting? Having set the standard in the desert, Jesus doesn't make a big deal about it. Fasting was a common practice, and there's no indication that he wanted it to end and that there was no longer any need for it. He did parody those who make a big show of fasting, contorting their faces in pain and making a public display of their self-denial, as if this in some way brings about divine favour. It doesn't.

Perhaps today, Jesus would be even more satirical about what Lent and Easter has become. Maybe he would begin by pointing to the day when Lent begins, Shrove Tuesday, so-called because one is obtaining absolution – or shriving – for one's sins. It's surely a short hop from there to calling it Pancake Day, using up the fat before the lean season of Lent. Other cultures are less subtle, calling that day 'Fat Tuesday', which has in turn morphed into gaudy Mardi Gras celebrations where the vibe seems to be 'Lent starts tomorrow so right now, let's behave like sailors on shore leave'. If Jesus has instituted Lent, I'm not sure this would be how he imagined the launch date looking.

And so we move on to the period of Lent itself and the token giving up of something, like a sugary cocoa product. In effect, Lent has become an excuse to have another swing at a New Year's Resolution. A second bite of the apple. The last chance saloon for will power. Somehow, Easter has become about self-improvement – when it is intended to bring about something quite different: a contrite and broken heart that cries out to the Lord for forgiveness and grace, rather than a forced smile wrapped around a low-fat sugar-free cereal bar.

Somehow, it is now appropriate to end this season of self-denial by gorging on chocolate eggs on Easter Sunday. How did this happen? Presumably the same way as the transformation of the celebration of the Birth of Christ with dragging a tree indoors, covering it in shiny balls, topping it off with a fairy (rather than an angel) and using mistletoe as social blackmail for getting a free kiss.

The chocolate Easter eggs are another oddity that we have come to accept as normal. But it can't have been part of the plan from Day 1, surely? It's a Monty Python scene when you think about it. Picture the Good Friday scene with Eric Idle as a thief on the cross leaning over to Jesus and saying 'I know you're omniscient and all that but here's one you won't see coming. In two thousand years' time, they'll remember your death on the cross and subsequent empty tomb by giving each other eggs made of chocolate. Some of them will have a free mug underneath. It's funny old world, eh?'

Doomsday

or: The upsides of Armageddon

This week, I learned that a strong belief held by most Christians for 2000 years is laughable. Literally. On the BBC panel-game *QI* recently, the idea of Jesus' return cropped up. The question was about The Great Disappointment of 1844 in which millions of Americans really believed that Jesus Christ would be returning very soon indeed. You probably know the end to this story. He did not return, much to the amusement of religious cynics and to Christians who'd actually read the Bible and realised that we do not know the day or the hour.

In rounding off this section on *QI*, Stephen Fry read out one of those wonderful jumping off points for all comedians, columnists and commentators. You know the one. It's the sentence that begins 'Seventy three per cent of Americans believe that ...' and you finish it off with something plainly unbelievable to liberal British secularists. Something about alien abduction, the reality of hell or the identity of the anti-christ normally works well. And then we can all enjoy a warm glow of superiority over a country that is essentially better at everything than us. And is more polite. While we're all chuckling, it's handy to forget that 50 per cent of Brits are not convinced about global warming and would at least consider voting for the BNP.

What these surveys reveal is that millions of perfectly pleasant and prosperous people have radically different worldviews and assumptions. Shaking one's head about people with these views and saying 'they must be out of their tiny minds' doesn't really get us anywhere. In this case, Mr Fry revealed that about 50 per cent of Americans believe that Jesus will return. Everyone chuckled at how silly Americans are for being so Christian and the quiz moved on.

What was most remarkable to me was the tone of all of the above wasn't so much sneering as astonished that anyone could ever have believed something so plainly daft as the Return of Jesus Christ. And it does sound rather potty when it's described – especially the physical description of The Rapture. But then anything described can easily sound ridiculous. Try explaining sex, childbirth or golf. I'm pretty sure they're all real, though. Moreover, scoffing is very easy, lots of fun to do and often fun to watch – hence 99 per cent of all TV panel games.

The other surprise was that the 50 per cent who believed that Jesus was returning seemed rather low given the active and passive Christianity in America. It's something that the British find impossible to comprehend. Presidents are expected to be broadly Christian. *The Simpsons* still go to Church – along with almost everyone else in Springfield. And part of that Christian package is Jesus' birth, death, resurrection and return.

And yet Christians in Britain are curiously reluctant to talk about that final act in the Christian story. Many are embarrassed by it, don't believe it, or theologise their way out of it. Most disliked doctrines are pinned on the apostle Paul, Jesus is vindicated and declared misunderstood, and we can all get on with our lives as if nothing has, or is about to, happen. Except on this issue, Jesus talked about returning quite a lot. The Return of Jesus, which sounds like an unimaginative sequel to the Bible, is deemed to be an unattractive part of Christianity and so, in an attempt to be liked, or less disliked, it is quietly dropped.

And yet, non-Christians don't seem to want a god who just lets things run and run, let alone a god who doesn't even know the future. They want judgement. Everyone does. If they can't find it in a religion, they look for it elsewhere. Football fans do it. Environmentalists do it. They wish judgement upon themselves and their community for sins committed. The football fan says 'I hope my team loses because until they pick McMahon, they'll never learn. Bring on relegation.' The environmentalist says 'We've plundered the planet for too long. Mankind needs to learn sustainability. Bring on catastrophe.'

We know we deserve judgement. We know we've made a mess. It's why Robin Williams speculated that Jesus won't return as a carpenter but a sheet-metal worker and he's going to be really angry. If we lose the message of judgement, we also jettison hope itself. Jesus doesn't just judge. He will remake a perfect glorious world. Isn't that something we all want?

Crosses to Bear

or: The intolerance of the inclusivity

Jesus was a very poor salesman. He regularly explained to anyone who would listen that following him would be, at best, embarrassing; at worst costly and painful. Not only do Christians have to endure the command to love each other – which is a lot harder than it sounds – but they also have to deny themselves, take up their cross and follow Him. When a man approached Jesus saying 'I will follow you, but first I must bury my father,' Jesus replied, 'Let the dead bury their own dead.' Smooth. One can imagine Peter or John standing next to him shaking their heads, tearing up another Disciple Application Form because another potential apostle has been scared off.

The popular image of Jesus, the meek, mild and witty John-Lennon-meets-Gandhi-type, could not be more different from the Jesus of the gospels who constantly warns about the dangers of hell, false religion, and money. Then, having told people His followers will be mocked, persecuted and possibly killed, He leads the way by being arrested, flogged, mocked and killed.

Given these numerous, stark warnings, it may be surprising then that Christians in Britain complain so much about their lot in life, especially given that their so-called persecution is so mild in comparison to what has been promised by Jesus – and as it is experienced by millions of Christians all over the world. Christian groups and agencies love to recycle articles from the newspapers that *another* Christian has been disciplined for saying grace at a meal or sacked for wearing an ichthus on their tie.

This is not to say that Christians should not speak up. There is much to be said for defending your Christian brother who is being marginalised because of their faith. Christians are right to call for the name of Jesus to be honoured and respected. But no one is quite sure what that looks like in a pluralistic, secular society.

Whenever I hear a story of a nurse being disciplined for wearing a cross or offering to pray, I look to see what the name of the hospital is – and smirk if it is a St Saviour's or a St Thomas's. Our entire hospital system is based on what was established by Christianity and monasticism in particular. To insist, therefore, that a nurse eschew all other vestiges of the faith is somewhat perverse. (These days, though, the nurse in question usually works for the South Staffordshire Primary Healthcare and Wellness Trust or some other boring, secular-sounding title, so the joke doesn't work as well.) That said, nurses are called 'sisters', a nod to a Christian past. This doesn't mean there should be Alpha Courses run in every ward but it does mean that Christianity should be accepted as legitimate and meaningful, even if some patients choose to ignore it.

It seems the problem here is not the vast majority who don't believe in Christianity but are happy to tolerate it, but a vocal secularist minority who hate Christianity because it is a dogmatic exclusive worldview. What they don't understand is that their secularism is not the blank canvas that they think it is. Secularism is also a dogmatic exclusive world view. It insists that faith must be private and erased from public view. How exclusive can you get?

Another irony is that the very concept of a hospital is a Christian one. Jesus himself led the way on caring for the weak, the sick and the marginalised, helping those who cannot help themselves. I have yet to understand why an ardent atheist who sees no story in creation, no point to life itself and views everything as a Nietzschean power-play would care whether the weak lived or died. A hospital run along Darwin/Dawkins lines would leave the frail and unproductive outside to perish whilst treating the minor ailments of the strongest and fittest (which rather defeats the point of a hospital).

The secularists have not won the day. Some would argue the shrillness of their cries implies they know they've already lost. I'm not so sure. But Christians would do well not only to look to Jesus but to Daniel and his friends. When they defied the orders of Nebuchadnezzar to follow the Lord, they did so knowing that they would receive an unjust lethal punishment. They did not whine that this was unfair, but accepted their fate because they deemed their faith to be worth dying for. If British Christians baulk at the odd tribunal, what are they really saying about their faith?

Bashing the Pope

or: The revelation of one of my guilty secrets

We all have favourite movies that are hard to justify on any artistic level, perhaps hidden away on DVD in a cupboard, nowhere near our critically acclaimed boxed set-collections. After all, a copy of *Police Academy 5: Assignment Miami Beach* would really ruin the effect of *West Wing*, and *The Wire* on our shelves.

One of my guilty secrets is *The Pope Must Die*, a splendidly silly romp from 1991 in which a humble priest played by Robbie Coltrane is made Pope owing to a clerical error. The film caused a minor ripple of controversy on release – not on the grounds that the movie showed the Vatican being in league with the Mafia, or that the Catholic Church was inherently corrupt or mean (Monsignor Fitchie: We're the Church. We collect money. We don't give it out). It was just felt the title was a bit much – so in America, the film was called *The Pope Must Diet*, even though there is almost no reference to His Holiness's size throughout the movie.

Given the current religious climate, a film of this nature would probably be much more profitable, although it's hard to imagine a movie like this being made today. It's far too affectionate. The sort of people who make films would really put the boot in.

This happened in 2004 in a controversial cartoon made for BBC3 called *Popetown*. It was essentially deemed not funny enough to justify the massive offence it would cause. The fact that the series wasn't very funny must have been a giant relief to the commissioners, which is an unusual situation. One wonders why they stopped applying this level of restraint in sparing us from other programmes that are both unfunny and offensive, e.g. *Insert name of your least favourite BBC3 comedy here (preferably not mine, thanks.)*

Pope Benedict XVI himself graced this island with his presence in 2010. It garnered mixed coverage. BBC gave the proceedings quite a lot of airtime. Some were offended by the coverage, saying that the whole thing has been largely sneery and prejudiced, giving far too much prominence to the relatively few protestors the Pope has attracted. Others have been offended that the Pope and the Catholic church has been given *any* airtime and hours of free publicity.

Clearly, the very existence of a Pope clearly got under the skin of normally intelligent, respectable people. Some talked about silly plans to try and arrest His so-called Holiness on arrival. It felt like those bombastic claims of school leavers who talk about what they'll do on their last day (*Yeah, like, I'll probably set fire to the sports hall or something?*). Professor Richard Dawkins, always good for a nuanced and sensible quotation about religion, said that if he were to meet Pope Benedict XVI – whom only ever refers to the pope as 'Mr Ratzinger' – he would say 'Go home to your tin pot Mussolini-concocted principality, and don't come back.'

The considerably nicer Stephen Fry did his best to argue that the Pope was, of course, welcome to come and address British Roman Catholics, but to call it a state visit is a sham, since the Vatican's not really a state. It is on paper. The 'tin-pot principality' was indeed established under Mussolini in 1929 but is hardly your run-of-the-mill European democracy. Perhaps Mr Fry could take the Vatican more seriously as a nation if they entered the Eurovision Song Contest. I would certainly find singing Cardinals to be a welcome addition to the already preposterous schedule.

Mr Fry's objection to the visit on these grounds is, however, a little disingenuous as his views about the Papcy were made very clear in a debate last year on whether the

Catholic Church is a force for good in the world. He got very cross indeed, making a speech that lots of other actors, comedians and anti-Catholic media-types would happily say 'amen' to.

They have grounds for criticising the Catholic Church that are so obvious and widely reported they are barely worth restating. But ultimately, Fry, Dawkins and their disciples are furious that the billion-strong Catholic Church has not changed its doctrine for hundreds of years to reflect current thinking and 21st century morality – or lack of. But what makes Fry and the others even more furious is that no matter what they say, how mean they are and how funny they are, it doesn't appear to make any difference at all. The Church goes on. It began with St Peter, weathered Erasmus, Luther and Calvin, *The Pope Must Die* and *Popetown*. Some twittering comedians aren't really anything to worry about.

Neo-Calvinists

or: Why John Calvin wasn't very good at being French

America has just seen off the Neo-Cons. But are they ready for the Neo-Calvinists? Noting the rise of preachers like John Piper and Mark Driscoll, *Time* Magazine says that Neo-Calvinism is Number 3 in their list of 'Top 10 ideas Changing the World Right Now' – 'Evangelicalism's latest success story, complete with an utterly sovereign and micromanaging deity ... and the combination's logical consequence, predestination.'

The year 2009 marked John Calvin's 500th birthday. You could have been forgiven for not noticing. It is no surprise this anniversary failed to spark a bunch of festivals, books and documentaries on the BBC (which assumes our appetite for programmes about Charles Darwin is insatiable). John Calvin is not, and has never been, what the media call 'sexy'. Why not?

Let's take a look at some of the other Reformation superstars, if you can call them that (you can't). Luther, the original and the best, defiantly nailed his 95 Theses to a church door. Take that, Pope. Tyndale was a covert Bible translator – strangled and burned for making the Bible available in English. Thomas Cranmer wrote the beautiful Book of Common Prayer. Zwingli died in battle. And Thomas More was the *Man for All Seasons* (okay he wasn't really a Protestant). Calvin is not in this Protestant pantheon. Why not?

Calvin seems dour, methodical and a bit scary. He is hardly your stereotypical Frenchman – the lover of food, wine and women. Many completely forget that he was French, since his name is forever associated with Geneva, hardly a party town. Calvin's name, then, has the reputation of dull Swiss efficiency. On top of this, Calvin was a lawyer. Not a renegade monk. Or a freedom fighter on the run. An i-dotting, t-crossing solicitor.

This combines in Calvin's much-praised, rarely-read *Institutes*. Calvin enthusiasts love to claim that it is highly readable and well worth the effort. But only a Calvinist would say that. There's no story or narrative, so it's hardly a page-turner. Nor is it a collection of C. S. Lewis-like essays. It's tightly woven, systematic theology. Even the title, *The Institutes*, causes mild drowsiness. Readers are advised not to operate heavy machinery after reading. Compare the *Institutes of the Christian Religion* with Luther's *On the Babylonian Captivity of the Church* or *Against the Murderous, Thieving Hordes of Peasants*. But *The Institutes* are 'good for you'. So is fish oil and fruit. I'm largely a consumer of neither. (Hence I'm large.)

It is, perhaps, these factors that explain Calvin's appeal to conservative Evangelicals – who gravitate towards systematic theology, doctrinal correctness, fish oil and fruit, and away from narrative and ambiguity. And being liked by conservative Evangelicals makes Calvin even less hip by association today.

But it is, perhaps, the doctrine of Predestination that is the final nail in the coffin of popularity. *Time* magazine implies this as it goes on. God's utter sovereignty is coupled with 'sinful and puny humanity, and the combination's logical consequence, predestination: the belief that before time's dawn, God decided whom he would save (or not), unaffected by any subsequent human action or decision.' The idea that man does not, and cannot, choose God, but that God chooses man is very humbling – even humiliating. For many, indeed most, it is too much.

The name John Calvin, then, needs some considerable PR to push Neo-Calvinism from 'influential' to 'hip'. Perhaps Geneva could build a Calvin theme park – Calvin Towers – in which those lucky enough to be sent tickets can enjoy the sights and sounds of Geneva 1549. Attend a meeting of the Consistory and get severely reprimanded for playing cards. (Buy a ticket for Calvin Towers and receive a discount on the Pennsylvanian theme-park Amish Land. Gasp and scream aboard the wooden horse-drawn rollercoasters.)

How about a biopic of Calvin's life? A four hour ecclesiastical courtroom drama starring Russell Crowe in the title role. It could be the film about the church–state divide that no one's been crying out for. What about a computer game? The makers of *Grand Theft Auto* could bring out a 1550 Edition, *Grand Horse Auto*. Ride a steed around the streets of Geneva, chewing tobacco, before returning the animal to its rightful owner with a few francs for compensation. How about a Calvin fragrance? *Predestination* – the unmistakeable smell of tulips that helps you remember the five points of Calvinism.

Maybe then the name of John Calvin will be great once more and we can finally ask the question – was Jesus a Calvinist?

Christian Festivals, Part 3: Easter

or: What's so Good about Friday?

Being an annual event, Good Friday doesn't seem particularly odd. And yet the reason the nation is granted an extra
day to wash the car and go and buy garden furniture at B&Q
is because Jesus Christ was crucified this Friday – the
Passover Friday – nearly two thousand years ago.

The passion story, and the crucifixion itself is not a pretty
scene. It is ugly, brutal and distressing. Jesus, an innocent
man, is flogged, whipped, spat on, forced to carry a cross,
then nailed to it, and hung up to die. It is an inventively cruel
mode of execution that is deeply unflattering to the society
that not only dreamed it up but carried it out many times.

There seems little Good about the Friday in question,
then. And it gets worse. It would be bad enough if this Jesus
of Nazareth were merely an innocent man. But he is not. He
is Jesus of Heaven too. When he was born, he was called
Emmanuel – which means 'God with us'. And we tried him,
beat him, mocked him and killed him. In the grand scheme
of things that is not a Good day. It is possibly the worst of all
days.

In one sense, Good Friday represents the darkest, strang-
est, sickest joke: God became man and walked the earth. He
made the lame walk, he made the blind see and he com-
manded storms with his voice. Even if you're not a Christian,
you have to admit that this man Jesus lived a wonderful life.

And yet our reaction two thousand years ago is depressing and unsurprising. We killed him. We didn't even do it in

private, hoping no one would notice, but in plain view of the world – with the authority of the religious community and the state.

What is even stranger about this event is that the Jesus Christ of the New Testament was able to raise people from the dead. Three such instances are testified. In the most famous case, in which he raised Lazarus who had been dead in the tomb for three whole days before being called out, many witnesses reported back to the Jewish authorities, who were furious and declared that Jesus would have to die. It seems a curious action plan to dispose of this troublesome man, given his astonishing resurrecting powers.

The crucifixion itself is steeped in all kinds of irony. Jesus was 'crowned' with a crown of thorns and royal robe put on him. A sign was written up saying 'This is the King of the Jews'. They all thought it a hilarious joke, and yet that is exactly what he was. True King of the Jews – a direct descendant from David and Abraham. Priests mocked Jesus saying 'He saved others, but he can't save himself!' But he could. He just chose not to. What is going on?

The clues are all there in the story. It is Passover. The day when God's people would slaughter a perfect lamb, daub the blood on the doorframe and escape the judgment of the angels – and, leaving behind their slavery to Pharaoh, to go freely into the land, to be the people that God made them to be.

By allowing himself to be slaughtered, Jesus showed himself to be the true lamb of the Passover, giving his life so that his people could escape the judgment that is referred to throughout the Bible; to live freely in the land, to be the people God made us to be. Jesus saves us from our slavery, from the madness of sin, rebellion and hatred, the kind of madness that blinds our eyes and makes us kill those with power, and opens truly blind eyes. Despite gruesome appearances, that day on which Jesus died, that Friday, was a very Good one.

Religion and Offence, Part 2: Swearing

*or: Mind your %$@*ing language*

It may surprise readers to learn that I am unable to make my living writing books like the one you currently hold in your hands. My day-job is sitcom writing, which is both very enjoyable, being fun, rewarding and mostly indoors.

The word 'sitcom' is a poor description of the genre. Situation comedies, when done well, are usually character comedies (although one can see that 'charcom' is a less pleasing word). The sitcom writer needs to be able to think like his characters, work out what they do in any given situation and write dialogue for them. And here we encounter a strange world of responsibility. Allow me to explain.

Recently, I've been working on a show in which some of the characters swear like troopers, for reasons that should be obvious if you watch the show. On watching, some members of my family would have been surprised at the words it turns out that I know – and how deftly I employ them as nouns, verbs and adjectives. My Christian friends will be equally surprised – and some of them not a little appalled, I suspect. The reason is that I sit within the Evangelical camp. It's a camp I'm broadly happy with. Our music may verge on the naff and our liturgy may be occasionally trite, but we like to think we're very comfortable with the Bible. However, the Evangelical camp takes a view on bad language: it is not just frowned upon, but tutted at.

There are two schools of thought when it comes to swearing and comedy. The first is that swearing simply isn't funny and that resorting to foul language is the mark of creative bankruptcy. The second – and more convincing – school of thought is that swearing can be very funny and that foul language can be pleasingly shocking and breathtakingly inventive. Stephen Fry, one of our greatest wordsmiths, argues that swearing is often done by those with large vocabularies, not the smallest. But quoting Stephen Fry is hardly going to win an argument with a fellow Evangelical.

It's no use my arguing that I wrote two scripts for two different sitcoms: one script was a 'gritty' show (that's TV-speak for 'full of swearing'); the other script was a charming and innocent comedy that contained no foul language, profanity or innuendo. I earnestly prayed that the latter show would be commissioned. And it wasn't. The 'gritty' show was the chosen one.

I could argue that when I write characters in fiction, I am writing words and actions for characters who say and do things that I would not say and do. Occasionally, my characters say things that I would say or agree with, but rarely. The Bible is full of people doing and saying things I do not agree with. Were the Bible writers wrong to write them so? Jesus told stories about foolish people doing foolish things. Was he wrong to tell such stories?

But we're talking specifically about swearing. And yet, here we see our Bible translators are much more prudish than the original authors. In the Old Testament, there's an expression to do with 'those that piss against the wall' (KJV), which occurs six times. It is fitting that the King James's version of the Bible should be bawdy. This was the king who, upon being told that the crowd wish to see his face, cried out 'God's wounds! I will pull down my breeches and they shall see my arse!' But more recently, NIV and ESV have euphemised these verses about mural urination.

Maybe you'd expect this kind of crudity in the Old Testament which is visceral and scatological. But there is strong language in the touch-feely-New-Testament too, not least on the lips of Jesus who not only used hyperbole, but outright insults when talking to Pharisees and those who exploited their position. His intention was to offend.

The Apostle Paul is a man who suggests the Judaisers, who like to circumcise Gentiles, go the whole way and cut off their entire manhood. And, some translators suggest that Paul considers his own life to be 'shit' compared to the surpassing worth of knowing Christ Jesus. It seems that we are perhaps more prudish than our Biblical heroes.

Perhaps the discomfort for Evangelicals is because strong language comes from genuine strong emotion – and this is not something we readily show. The average British Evangelical Male is a triple helping of cold fish. And yet the Bible is full of passionate speech. Perhaps this is what it really means to let your conversations be salty.

Questions! Questions!

or: How to have a constructive discussion about religion

I hope future generations will look back on our version of the internet without too much disdain. They will laugh our primitive iPhones, and our incessant tweets and, most of all, our bizarre insistence on allowing people to leave comments about everything.

This comment facility does give the reader the chance to challenge an article that they find ill-informed, prejudiced or just plain wrong. Normally, though, they give the reader an opportunity the chance to appear even more ill-informed, prejudiced and wrong than the author. This is an impressive feat when the author of the original piece is Johann Hari or Quentin Letts.

Religion attracts particularly vehement lunacy from right across the spectrum. But the most prevalent and infuriating comments are the ones by the casual atheist based on nothing but received opinions and knee-jerk lazy stereotypes. Comments like 'ReggieBoy97: Religion's just stupid. Anyone who prays to any 'god' has been brainwashed.' Or 'BasterdSonofSammyDavisJr: The Bible's a load of cack, full of dumb laws, violence and contradictions. FAIL." If I had the time or inclination, here's the comment I'd like to post in response to the ones above:

'Well done, BasterdSonofSammyDavisJr! You and your towering intellect have seen through our religious sham. How did you do it? Even though 99.9% of all people who have ever lived have been religious in some way, it's amazing that you and

ReggieBoy97, have realised that the emperor has no clothes and that religion is, and always has been, stooooopid (sic). And to put this truth so succinctly in one fraction of your lunch-hour taken at the desk of the call-centre you work in was impressive. Have you considered a career in academia? And as for you, BasterdSonofSammyDavisJr – you've certainly put thousands of years of intense Biblical scholarship into perspective and put to shame the great minds of the past who have taken the Bible seriously, (Newton, Aquinas, C. S. Lewis, etc.). After all, the Bible was written by lots of different people in different languages and cultures over the course of a thousand years. It should be an easy read, yeah? And have no textual problems at all. Besides, if 'God' was serious about communicating, he would have just beamed down golden tablets of instructions which someone could copy before they vanished so that we don't make the mistake of worshipping the tablets. That is much more plausible. Keep up the good work everyone:-)'

I'd like to say these things because I'm impatient, I think I'm funny and I'm not very nice. But heavy sarcasm, however, will get us nowhere (other than making me feel a whole lot better). That said, Jesus (who was patient, genuinely funny and really nice) did employ heavy sarcasm to good effect in the face of Pharisees. For example in Mark 7, Jesus effectively says 'Ooh, I'm loving the way you set aside the commandments of God so you can do your own thing'. Zing.

But Jesus uses another technique which is much more polite, and therefore more devastating. He answers hostile questions with his own questions. This very idea fills some evangelicals with dread, since questions invite dialogue, and dialogue invites conversation which could imply that truth is in some way negotiated rather than proclaimed, defended, restated, said again slightly louder and then illustrated, ideally with paints on whiteboard and easel.

I would agree that a sermon should be stated, rather than chaired, but oranges are not the only fruit. Questions and conversations are a particularly rabbinic way of going about things and Jesus was Jewish (remember?).

Questions reveal motives, which can be useful. A colleague once asked me 'Don't you think the Bible needs
updating?' I was tempted to launch into a lengthy defence of
the historicity of the Gospels with a few thoughts on the
Apocrypha thrown in. Instead, I asked her 'What would you
like the Bible to say?' She said that the Bible contained
nothing on the subject of abortion. That was what she really
wanted to talk about. I was very glad to have found that out.
And it informed our on-going discussion.

The power of the question is truly astonishing. The
shorter the better. If you're asked 'Don't you think religion is
just brainwashing?' try answering 'Which one?' If you're
asked 'Don't you think all religions worship the same God?',
you could reply 'Really? But aren't they so different?' This
might gently reveal to them that they need to think this
through a little more. Asked, 'Isn't the Bible is full of contradictions?' you could answer by asking 'Which bit?'

We live in a world which has lots of questions for the
Church. And questions work better when there's genuine
dialogue – and yet Christians (especially my Evangelical
kind) often seem intent on monologue. While this situation
remains, no one's going to be listening to our answers. This
needs to change.

It's Your Funeral

or: Ill-advised song choices as you leave this mortal coil

As a nation, we don't do death well. In other countries, widows, completely dressed in black, scream and wail over the coffin of their loved one. There is howling and gnashing of teeth. In Britain, people prefer to play James Blunt's 'Goodbye My Lover', which one may have thought would produce a similar hysterical effect.

Every year, the UK Bereavement Register's Annual Survey publishes a 'Top of the Popped Cloggs'. Blunt, who penned the lyric 'I know you well, I know your smell' is this year's number one. It is not clear how James Blunt feels about writing music that people would like to be played after they are dead; music to be cremated by.

Blunt recently pushed 'Angels' to number two; Take That, Robbie. 'I've Had the Time of my Life' from *Dirty Dancing* is three, followed by Bette Midler's 'Wind' which she still insists is beneath her wings. Jesus and Mozart combine forces in 'Pie Jesu', which only makes it to Number 5.

It seems odd that people should request a pop song to be played at their funeral, subjecting a church full of people to something like 'My Heart Will Go On.' Why do they do that, unless it's one last act of revenge on the relatives? The problem, apart from the inevitable naffness, is that pop songs are not written to be played at funerals. Their lyrics never quite fit. Also in the top ten is 'Every Breath You Take', which is only suitable for someone who's been bumped off by their stalker. Otherwise, it doesn't really tie up.

This odd propensity for secular music at funerals is a sign of how de-churched Britain has become. In the last census, 41 million people ticked the box marked 'Christian', when they had the option saying they were of no religion (or Jedi). And yet Sundays see less than 4 million in church; 37 million people would only be seen dead in Church. In a casket.

We are living in a post-religious society and these songs are the panic alarms. 'Argh! What do we do in church? No idea! Play some Yazz – 'The Only Way is Up!' This is partly the fault of the faithful who have done their best to make church a bizarre, pew-based spectacle, offering British Christianity rather than the Gospel of Jesus Christ. We have priests in strange outfits – when there is no real biblical justification for priestliness (see Hebrews, *passim*) or robes, copes, stoles, albs, chasubles or any other kind of clerical poncho. Yes, each garment is very symbolic; but if you don't know the symbolism, they just look weird. But the English are comfortable with the vicars in dog collars, and bishops in purple shirts and daft hats. It means they can be conveniently filed under 'Sweet English Eccentrics'.

Similarly, the 'after-life' theology that many non-Christians have in their heads about the semi-Christian heaven is just a hotchpotch of imagery taken from the Bible, represented in Renaissance art, than blended into some soothing jumble of St Peter, the Pearly Gates, white light, harps, angels, clouds and wings. Like a quasi-religious card from Clinton's. Sadly, the result isn't in the least bit attractive. So why would you steal these images of a nebulous, nirvana-style heaven when you're missing out on the reality of a true biblical picture of heaven? It's like breaking into the British Museum, walking past the Rosetta Stone, and stealing the novelty pens from the gift shop.

The TV sketch version of heaven is perpetuated in the media because it's exactly that. A TV sketch; a convenient, non-threatening after-life shorthand. The Simpsons use it. Films like *Bruce Almighty* tap into it. (And if anyone's going to 'play God', I suppose it would have to be Morgan Freeman.)

Every day, people tell Pearly Gates jokes, as if a series of one-liners with St Peter is going to bring about entry into heaven. Christians frequently tell such jokes but in so doing, continue the myth that our eternal destiny is in some way negotiable by us. It is not. In fact, the pearly gates have become disconnected from the Biblical reality. Comedian Ross Noble talks about the Pearly Gates as being of little use if there isn't a pearly wall, suggesting that Hitler and Mussolini could sneak into heaven round the side.

The heaven promised in the Bible is real and physical, perfect and wonderful. Every tear wiped away; no more death or suffering. We'll all be in perfect relationship with God and each other in the New Jerusalem. Isn't that more appealing than sitting on a cloud with a harp next to a podgy baby with wings? Of course it is. But do Christians present a heaven which is bristling with goodness and beauty? I'm not sure we do. This is surprising given that our world is so clearly damaged and dysfunctional. Are Christians guilty of trying to fix the current creation at the expense of telling non-Christians about the new perfect one?

Nothing freaks out non-Christians more than a proper Christian funeral, where life is celebrated; friends and family don't wistfully talk about the deceased 'going to a better place' or 'playing on the big golf course in the sky' but confidently claim a place with God in heaven, as Christians can. Who needs 'Bright Eyes' or 'Memory', which are songs about rabbits and cats, when the whole congregation can sing something stunning, meaningful and appropriate like 'Amazing Grace'? There is no need for naff sentimentality where there is confidence and conviction.

That's Britain. For sheer nihilism, you have Europe where the top five Bereavement best-sellers feature Queen's 'The Show Must Go On' and, most worryingly, 'Highway to Hell' by AC/DC. You've got to admire their post-Christian honesty.

The Princess Phenomenon

or: Why we all need a knight in shining armour

My daughter is four and likes pink. She likes to wear dresses and tiaras and wants to be a princess. This is no great surprise. And yet this phenomenon angers some people, like Laura Penny in the *New Statesman* (*New Statesperson*, by now, surely?). She blames the $4bn Disney Princess industry. I have no idea what Disney Princess she is referring to – since our daughter doesn't really watch Disney at the moment. All I do know is that Disney have recently acquired Lucasfilm, which means lots of storm troopers and Jedi knights, but also one more Princess, in the form of Leia.

I don't think my daughter has a favourite Disney princess. But she likes to dress up as a princess (which overlaps with being a fairy, an angel and a ballerina) and, when she has to wear trousers, she is sad because, in her own words 'Princesses don't wear trousers'.

This phenomenon in my daughter seems to have emerged organically. We never pushed the 'Princess Experience', but we don't see any need to crush it, distract her from it or frantically promote something else. I suspect that in ten years' time, she will be rather bored of princesses and have moved on to ponies or pop music. Or playing the piano, painting or Purcell.

So why the eye-rolling at the desire of little girls – and big girls – to be a princess? Like most enduring images, and romantic tales, it gets to the heart of what it is to be human.

It is generally good advice to tell a young girl that hoping to marry a prince is not a sensible life-plan. But most young girls probably know this. There just aren't enough princes to go round. What is the cause of the yearning? Surely it is a desire to be loved, cherished and adored? Who doesn't want that?

We can pretend that men and women are identical in every way, ignoring the fact that men can't ovulate or give birth. We could pretend that men and women are emotionally identical in every way, and that the desire to be a princess is purely the capitalist conditioning of the Disney corporation. But we know this is simply not true. Tales of princesses, princes, knights, dragons and maidens are ancient and timeless and permeate many cultures throughout the ages.

Likewise, we could pretend that acknowledging the differences means that one is superior to the other, or descend to other childish debates. Or we can conclude that the Princess phenomenon demonstrates there is clearly an enduring, even eternal, desire within many women to be beautiful, to be loved and cherished – just as there is a desire in many men to be strong, to protect and be respected, like a knight in shining armour.

So what are we to make of the promotion of Kate Middleton to the ranks of royalty? She was a 'common' girl, who has become a Princess. Laurie Penny argues that 'the cult of princesshood is, at root, a cult of social mobility'. She is right. The pleasant but unremarkable Kate Middleton has found favour with a prince – and now she is a Duchess, and may one day be Queen. The celebration of this tale is, for some, a denigration of the virtues of effort, industry and application, albeit framed in a feminist narrative. Why celebrate the unmerited favour of a prince?

And yet, unmerited favour is something we all cry out for. Little girls want to be princesses who are cherished. Little boys want to be knights who are respected. And we crave these things because we know in our heart of hearts that we are unworthy of them. These stories are so successful because they tap into that unfulfilled desire.

In some ways, this is why Christianity is so hard to stomach – because it is about finding unmerited favour with a Prince, in this case, Jesus. (This is not a great surprise, either) The Christian is not someone who, by character or hard work, is worthy of Christ's approval, love and sacrifice – but the recipient of those things. If we want those royal spiritual robes – and the acceptance and respect on offer – hanging around the palace or demanding to be let in will be a fruitless endeavour.

Our response may be to turn away, and decide we don't want the approval of anyone, and that we only need to justify our lives and ambitions to ourselves. But ultimately, if we do that, we will find that we are left with the harshest and most unjust and unforgiving task master of all – ourselves.

Some kind of Conclusion to All of the Above – Death by Civilisation

or: How to accidentally ruin a perfectly decent society (and how it might still be saved)

> *'Dear friends, let us love one another, for love comes from God.'*
> John (from the Bible)

In 1066, England was stolen. There was a famous battle near Hastings. Harold Godwinson was killed and William of Normandy took his throne. But that's not how he stole England. Maybe the throne was rightfully William's, although those who actually lived in England at the time seemed to disagree, but it is what happened next that was wrong.

By 'next' I mean The Doomsday Book. At first glance, a Book of Everything seems like a good and useful thing to write. William was new in town and wanted to find out who owned what. But this giant audit was not for tax purposes. It was for legitimising the astonishing land-grab that was the Norman Conquest. Land had been seized and reallocated at the whim of the king, who was able to declare who owned what. Saxon landowners were effectively made tenants of their own land, paying rent to a Norman overlord who, in turn, paid their dues to the King, by whose authority they had that land.

The new king overturned basic property rights to suit his own ends, consolidate his rule and feather his nest. He stole England. It's surprising that he isn't widely despised. But in a sense, we are so inured to the over-reaching arm of the State that what he did does not seem all that bad. In his defence, William the Conqueror stole the country once. Our current government takes half of the country's money every year and has done for decades. Although our personal taxation is almost certainly lower than 50 per cent, all other taxes and duties add up to ensure that the government's overall tax revenue is about half of our GDP.

I am not saying that this situation is a gross injustice *per se*. We have voted for this government and for other governments that were very similar. But our children have not. They are the ones who will face the gross injustice of paying off the hundreds of billions of pounds of debt recent governments have amassed. They will also foot the bill for the pensions that the older generations have promised each other. Our government, with our permission, is stealing – but it is stealing from our children.

How have we got into this mess? And all the messes highlighted in this book? I return to the general thesis of the book – that institutions tend to make things worse. But let us nuance this thesis. Institutions have their place. We need the State, Markets, the Media, Academia and the Church. But we apply them incorrectly with the wrong expectations.

This is because we routinely misdiagnose our problems. We ask the State to ban things we don't like and fund things we want. We want the State to teach our children how to live and think in schools. We want to co-opt the Media to force the State to raise taxes or pass laws to solve our problems. We demand that the Markets provide money for this – but when the Markets themselves fail, we demand the State intercede. We also want Academia and science to find answers for our problems, create cures and produce panaceas. And on top of this, we want social mobility, the freedom to choose our own destiny, and healthcare that is free at the point of use.

We can have lots of these things. But our problem is that we want them on humanist or secular terms. We think we can fix everything without making moral judgments. In fact, we are now insistent that we should not make moral judgments. As a society, we are so convinced The Church has nothing to offer, we are forced to use the large blunt instruments of The State and The Markets to fix our ills – and it doesn't work. Allow me to take an example: binge drinking.

Teenagers and young people get very drunk in public, having previously gotten drunk in private earlier that evening. They swarm around our city centres on Thursday, Friday and Saturday nights, falling over, being sick and rude. Our society doesn't like this. But we don't want to make a moral judgment, so we have to say that we don't like binge drinking because it is anti-social and expensive. Every social problem has to be categorised as an economic one. Binge drinkers can cause criminal damage to council/state property (£), will be unable to hold down jobs and need state benefits (££) and will suffer long-term health problems that the state will have to pay for (£££).

Drunkenness is indeed a social and financial problem, but it is principally a moral one. But we cannot admit this and make this a debate about morality or religion. Instead, we go reaching for the overbearing institutions to fix the problem. The popular solution to binge drinking is, apparently, raising the price of alcohol because the market has made it too cheap. So the State is to use its power to intervene in the market to make alcohol more expensive. Do we really think the cold hand of the market and the strong arm of the state will deal with a problem like this?

What does the church have to offer in a situation like this? I'm not arguing that the Church should stand up and denounce drunkenness (although saying this sort of thing now and then probably wouldn't hurt). I am saying that teenagers getting out of their minds on alcohol until they need their stomachs pumped on a regular basis is not just an economic problem. What would Jesus do? He would be out on the streets, talking to these teenagers – listening, responding, helping and challenging.

And that is what happens in my home town. Local churches have clubbed together to have teams wander the streets late at night to help those who've lost their way. This may not seem like much, but these Christians can offer the one thing we need, and the only thing the state and the market cannot provide – Love.

The state can give you money or a house, but this is not an act of generosity. You are entitled to these things by dint of your birth in this country – or subsequent settlement in it. Likewise, if you fall on hard times, the market does not care. The market is sociable, but selfish. It has very cold hands. Similarly, the media is not your real friend, and a science experiment has no soul.

This is why this fifth realm, The Church, the odd, over-looked, out-of-touch Church is the most important of all, with its dusty old Bible that is, somehow, the bestselling book in human history – so maybe there's something in it. And as the Church teaches society from this Bible, we will find the origins of that unconditional love that we need more than anything else.

'Dear friends, let us love one another, for love comes from God … This is how God showed his love among us: He sent his one and only Son into the world that we might live through him. This is love: not that we loved God, but that he loved us and sent his Son as an atoning sacrifice for our sins. Dear friends, since God so loved us, we also ought to love one another … If we love one another, God lives in us and his love is made complete in us.' (1 John 4:7–12)